BT
$4.56

# THE
## *OCCASIONAL VERSE*
### OF
# RICHARD STEELE

# PROLOGUE

## TO THE

## Univerſity of *OXFORD*.

Written by Mr.*Steel*, and ſpoken by Mr.*Wilks*.

AS wandring Streams by ſecret Force return
    To that capacious Ocean whence they're born;
    So for their Doom their Toils our Poets bring
    To the great OXFORD—where they learnt to ſing:
Then let the Learn'd their Viſit not refuſe,
Since what from you they gain, from us they looſe.
For when around the Sacred Place we range,
Our Admiration we for Knowledge change.
We leſs adore their more exalted Vein,
And muſt expeƈt a *Blenheim* or *Campaign*.
Such happy Seats wou'd rudeſt Minds inſpire,
And all that ſee muſt feel Poetick Fire.
Aſpiring Columns here, here beauteous Fields,
Here all that Art, here all that Nature yields;
Groves, Theatres, high Domes, and humble Shades,
Bright Palaces, and intermingl'd Glades
Make the admiring Traveller debate,
Whether they're formed for Solitude or State:
While empty Pomp th' Inhabitants deſpiſe,
With whom alone—'tis Greatneſs to be Wiſe.
Oh happy! and your Happineſs who ſee!
Where Innocence and Knowledge can agree!
Ye calm Speƈtators of a guilty Age,
Pity the Follies of the World and Stage;
Free from what either aƈt or repreſent,
Weigh both the Charaƈter and the Intent,
And know—Men as they are, our Authors drew,
But what they ſhou'd be we muſt learn from you.

*London*, Printed for BERNARD LINTOTT at the *Croſs-Keys* next
*Nando's* Coffee-Houſe near *Temple-Bar*. 1706.

Price 2*d*.

# THE

# *OCCASIONAL VERSE*

## OF

# RICHARD STEELE

Edited by

RAE BLANCHARD

AC. DOM INVS ILLV MINA TIO MEA OX.

*OXFORD*

AT THE CLARENDON PRESS

MCMLII

*Oxford University Press, Amen House, London E.C. 4*

GLASGOW NEW YORK TORONTO MELBOURNE WELLINGTON
BOMBAY CALCUTTA MADRAS CAPE TOWN

*Geoffrey Cumberlege, Publisher to the University*

PRINTED IN GREAT BRITAIN

# PREFACE

THIS is the fourth volume to appear since 1932 in my edition of the writings of Richard Steele. Although of less importance than other volumes in the series, it nevertheless seems to me to increase our understanding of his personality and genius. His verse-writing has been an unexplored chapter, very little thought ever having been given to the relation between his obvious interest in poets and poetry and his own practice, and no attempt ever made to collect his poems.

Of the helpfulness of many friendly persons during the preparation of the book, I can make here only a general acknowledgement; but for various kinds of assistance—both expert and practical—I wish to acknowledge publicly indebtedness to my co-worker John Loftis, a colleague Alice Braunlich, and my sister Neal Touchstone.

I have enjoyed the use of books and manuscripts and the generous help of librarians at the Library of the Peabody Institute in Baltimore; the Folger Library and the Library of Congress in Washington; the Boston Public Library; the Houghton Library at Harvard University; the William Andrews Clark Memorial Library in Los Angeles; the Chetham Library in Manchester; and, above all, the Henry E. Huntington Library in San Marino.

The book was finished during a six-months' visit at the Huntington in 1950. Only those who have been readers there will be able to understand that no praise, however extravagant, can describe adequately the greatness of the collection, the completeness of the reference materials, and the beauty of the surroundings in which one works. Godfrey Davies, Director of Research there, has my special gratitude.

I thank the Delegates of the Clarendon Press for permission to reprint the notes (revised) of 'The Songs in Steele's Plays', my contribution to *Pope and His Contemporaries: Essays Presented to George Sherburn*, 1949.

R. B.

BALTIMORE, MARYLAND
*1 January 1952*

# CONTENTS

INTRODUCTION . . . . . xiii

THE PROCESSION. A POEM ON THE FUNERAL OF
QUEEN MARY . . . . . 3

EPISTLES AND POEMS OF COMPLIMENT

To the Mirrour of British Knighthood . . 11
To Congreve on *The Way of the World* . 12
To Dr. Ellis . . . . . 14
The Sixth Ode of Horace applied to the Duke of
Marlborough . . . . 14
Verses addressed to Addison on the tragedy of
*Cato* . . . . . 15

THE SONGS IN THE PLAYS

*The Funeral* . . . . . 19
Let not Love on me bestow . . . 19
Ye Minutes bring the happy Hour . . 19
Cynderaxa Kind and Good . . . 19
On Yonder Bed supinely laid . . 20
Arise, arise great Dead . . . 20

*The Lying Lover* . . . . 21
Thou soft Machine (To Celia's Spinet) . 21
Venus has left her Grecian Isles . . 21
Since the Day of poor Man . . . 22
The rolling Years the Joys restore . . 22

*The Tender Husband* . . . . 23
See, Britons, see with Awful Eyes . . 23

With Studied Airs, and practis'd Smiles . 25
Why lovely Charmer, tell me why . . 25
While Gentle Parthenissa walks . . 26

*The Conscious Lovers* . . . . 26
From Place to Place forlorn I go . . 26

SHORT POEMS, EPIGRAMS, &c.

Verses on Mrs. Selwyn, being Valentine . 32
To a Young Lady who had Marry'd an Old Man 32
Song (Me Cupid made a Happy Slave) . 33
Epigrams: Adaptations of Martial . . 33
  Lib. 1. Ep. 13 . . . . 33
  De Vetula . . . . . 34
  Lib. 1. Ep. 68 . . . . 34
  Lib. 4. Ep. 22 . . . . 34
Toasts for the Kit-Cat Club . . . 35
Song (By what Power did she enslave me) . 35

PROLOGUES AND EPILOGUES

Prologue and Epilogue to *The Funeral* . . 39
Prologue and Epilogue to *The Lying Lover* . 41
Epilogue to *The Tender Husband* . . 42
Prologue to *The Mistake* . . . 43
Prologue to the University of Oxford . . 45
Prologue to *The Distrest Mother* . . 46
Prologue to *Lucius King of Britain* . . 47
Prologue intended for the players at Hampton Court . . . . . 49
Prologue intended for *All for Love* revived . 50

Epilogue to the Town intended to be spoken in 1721 . . . . . 51

Prologue and Epilogue to *Tamerlane* revived . 53

MISCELLANEA

To Dr. Hoadly . . . . 57

To Mrs. Manley . . . . 57

Rhymes in the Plays . . . . 57

Lines for a Poem by Another Hand . . 58

Lyric for Italian Music . . . 59

TENTATIVE ATTRIBUTIONS TO STEELE

Anacreontique to Delia on New-Years-Day. By Mr. S—— . . . . 63

On His Mistress. By a Parson . . . 63

Love's Relief . . . . . 64

To Belinda . . . . . 65

To Flavia . . . . . 65

On Nicolini's Leaving the Stage . . 65

Prologue Design'd for Mr. D——'s Last Play. By Several Hands . . . . 66

Prologue at the Opening of the Theatre-Royal the Day after His Majesty's Publick Entry . 68

Prologue Spoken at the Sensorium on His Majesty's Birthday . . . . 69

NOTES ON INDIVIDUAL POEMS . . . 73

POEMS OF DOUBTFUL AUTHORSHIP

Occasion'd upon Sight of Mrs. N——n . 109

Prisca's Advice to Novinda . . . 109

Novinda's Answer to Prisca . . . 110

On The Countess of B—wt—r's Recovery . 112

To the Queen; upon the Death of His Royal Highness . . . . . 112

To a Lady on Her Parrot . . . 113

A Song (Belinda, see from yonder flowers) . 114

From Anacreon. To a Painter: How to Paint his Beloved . . . . . 114

A Song (Tell me, Miranda, why should I) . 114

An Ode to Freedom . . . . 114

To Serena: on Presenting her *The Conscious Lovers* . . . . . 115

Epitaph on Tom D'Urfey . . . 115

LOST POEMS NOT FOUND

A Prologue to the Town Spoken at Lincoln's Inn Fields Theatre on 22 April 1720 . 116

Projected Prologues . . . . 117

POEMS WRONGLY ATTRIBUTED TO STEELE

Two Lapland Love Songs . . . 119

The Croxall 'Spencer Poems' . . . 119

Epilogue Spoken at the Censorium on the King's Birthday . . . . . 120

Prologue to *The Conscious Lovers*. Spoken in Dublin . . . . . 121

Orpheus Redivivus: A Poem on the Irish Harp 122

INDEX OF FIRST LINES . . . . 125

GENERAL INDEX . . . . . 129

# LIST OF ILLUSTRATIONS

PROLOGUE TO THE UNIVERSITY OF OXFORD. 1706.
Broadside No. 94 of the Halliwell-Phillipps Collection. Chetham Library, Manchester    .        . *frontispiece*

THE PROCESSION. A Poem on Her Majesties Funeral.
1695. Title-page of the first issue of Steele's first
publication. Reproduced from the copy in the Henry
E. Huntington Library, San Marino, California    .    *page* 1

INDIANA'S SONG IN THE CONSCIOUS LOVERS. Broadside No. 1489 of the Halliwell-Phillipps Collection.
Chetham Library, Manchester (*see* p. 87)    .    *page* 27

THE MUSES MERCURY: or, Monthly Miscellany.
February, 1707. Title-page of the copy in the
William Andrews Clark Memorial Library, Los
Angeles .    .    .    .    .    .    *page* 31

POETICAL MISCELLANIES . . . Publish'd by Mr. Steele.
1714 (*see* Introduction p. xix)    .    .    .    *page* 67

Ornaments reproduced from early editions of Steele's
plays .    .    .    .    .    *pages* xxiv, 70, 123

# INTRODUCTION

STEELE made his contribution in verse to the literature of the theatre. Very little can be said for any of his poems; there is only slight evidence that he paid much heed to them himself. But because of his great love for everything pertaining to the theatre—plays, writers of plays, actors, audiences, stagecraft, and playhouse management—we may believe that in retrospect he would have taken pride in the knowledge that the play-songs and prologues and epilogues gave pleasure to several generations of readers and playgoers in the eighteenth century. And though these minor verse forms no longer have even popular appeal, he might approve of seeing them altogether in a book like this one. The fourteen incidental songs written and set for his plays helped to carry into his century the tradition of the Restoration theatre song, and the sixteen or seventeen prologues and epilogues place him among the half-dozen most productive writers of that small literary genre between Dryden and Garrick.

Much of the remaining verse was written for occasions, and most of the poems may be characterized as period pieces: the commendatory epistle to a fellow playwright, lines written on the fly-leaf of a presentation copy, the valentine, the toast, the funeral poem, the Martial epigram, the Horatian ode, the Anacreontic, the short satiric poem, the light love-song. There is reason to believe that he wrote a good many more pieces than he was willing to acknowledge. The verse he had the talent and inclination to write doubtless seemed trivial in comparison with the poetical achievement of his contemporaries and frivolous, possibly, in the light of his own serious social purpose. He was perfectly aware that his gift was for prose. The long didactic poem he might have written took the form of periodical paper or moral tract; the political ballad, of a short pamphlet; the poetical Whig panegyric, of a dedicatory epistle for a volume of *Tatler, Spectator,* or *Guardian.* But though hidden the poetic impulse was there. There can be no doubt of his critical interest in poets and poetry. Together with Addison and other writers of the *Spectator* he is given credit for driving out the style of light verse in vogue during the latter years of the seventeenth century and for forming new fashions and a new taste. The list of contemporary writers whose poetry he presented to his reading public—quoted, analysed, advertised, and recommended—is certainly impressive. It was in his *Tatler* and *Spectator* papers that new poems by Pope, Swift, and Philips made their first appearance; new poems by Young and Gay were the subject of his papers in the *Guardian* and *Englishman*; Isaac Watts's paraphrase of the Scriptures found a place in the *Spectator*; John Hughes, Laurence Eusden, and Leonard Welsted, personal friends, were, of course, heartily encouraged, poems of the latter in *Town-Talk*; Garth, Harrison, Rowe, and Prior were all quoted by him and held up as representative of new trends. 'Addison's immortal verse' in *The Campaign* he spoke of with reverence. But, though acknowledging that 'the laborious epic strain' was beyond his powers, he celebrated the Blenheim victory in his own way—and at once, the Horatian ode preceding the more ambitious poem by a month. From his editorial introductions in the *Tatler* to Swift's poems *A Description of the Morning* and *A Description of a City Shower*, we see that he was quick to grasp the originality and newness of Swift's gift for satiric realism: '[he] has run into a way perfectly new and described things exactly as they happen.' Congreve's powers as dramatist and poet were celebrated in both verse and prose; but it was perhaps Congreve's excellence in the minor forms of verse which Steele himself attempted that kept him humble: 'That gentle, free, and easie Faculty, which also in Songs, and short Poems, You possess above all others, distinguishes it self whereever it appears.'

Other poets than his contemporaries were of interest to

Steele; and by observing his preferences we may possibly learn something about the ideals for his own verse-writing. The most numerous references scattered through his writings are as might be expected to Shakespeare's plays and *Paradise Lost*. Neither is the *Faerie Queene* forgotten. And respect for 'that great Master Dryden' is manifested in many quotations from the plays, prologues, and political satires. Certain poets of the seventeenth century in those years beginning to be thought old-fashioned, for example Donne, Butler, Oldham, Flatman, also had his allegiance and were drawn upon at one time and another to illustrate a point in taste or morals. The favourites, however, can be narrowed to a small homogeneous group whose volumes he read in the 1680's and 90's when he was growing up and his taste was being formed: Cowley, Denham, Suckling, and Rochester belong to this inner circle, and the idol of his youth seems to have been Waller.

When in a letter to Lady Steele he refers to 'your beloved Cowley', he is speaking for himself as well; and though 'the paper of Wit' mentioned may refer to a prose essay, Cowley to him was also 'a great poet'. The passage from *Of Greatness* beginning 'If e'er ambition did my fancy cheat' is quoted in both *Tatler* and *Spectator* papers, as also are lines from *The Waiting-Maid* and *Of Obscurity*; and in a *Lover* paper *On the Death of Sir Anthony Vandike* is excerpted. 'I always read Mr. Cowley with the greatest pleasure', Steele said from the heart. Quotations from Suckling's letters and from his poems *A Soldier* and *Upon Two Sisters* are found in the *Tatler* and *Lover*. An excerpt from Denham's *Destruction of Troy* was given prominence in the *Englishman*, and a favourite couplet from *Cooper's Hill* was quoted in the *Spectator* and served as a motto for a *Theatre* paper. Certain passages in Rochester's poem *A Letter from Artemisa in the Town to Cloe in the Country* seemed to be indelibly impressed upon his mind: for example the couplet beginning 'The Cordial-drop Heav'n in our Cup has thrown', which he first used in the *Christian Hero* and again years later in the *Lover*; the lines

'Who names that lost thing love' in two *Tatler* papers;
and so frequently that it became a part of his own thought,
'Love the most generous passion of the mind'. A half-
dozen lines from Rochester's *Allusion to Horace: Satire 1.
10* beginning 'Sedley has that prevailing art' were also
quoted many times—in two *Spectator* papers, in a letter to
Pope, and in the late, unfinished play *The School of Action*.

Waller, however, was the one whom he seemed to know
by heart and whose occasional poems, love lyrics, and
songs came most readily to mind for reference or illustra-
tive purpose. The favourites are cited again and again,
such poems as *Under a Lady's Picture*, *Upon the Death of
My Lady Rich*, *Of Love*, *The Battle of the Summer Islands*,
*Of the Marriage of the Dwarfs*, *For Drinking of Healths*,
and *On My Lady Isabella Playing on the Lute*. The qualities
Steele discerned in Waller's poetry and liked were his
simplicity of design, his grace and ease of manner, his lack
of obscenity, and, in the panegyrics, his romantic idealism.
We may even believe that Waller was the model more or
less consciously imitated in Steele's earliest verse—the
play-songs, the Anacreontic to Delia, 'Me Cupid made a
happy slave', *To a Young Lady Who Had Marry'd an Old
Man*, and the panegyric verses to Congreve and Marlborough. Nevertheless it would be a mistake to think that
he began exactly where Waller had left off. Touches of
humour and eagerness for fun, unlike Waller and peculiar
to Steele, are to be found even in the early poems of love
and gallantry.

A satirical note characterizes the kind of short poem
that Steele liked most in the poetry of his contemporaries;
at least that is the implication in his criticism of a poem
by Lady Winchilsea and another by Congreve. Both dis-
sect the follies of womankind with a light touch of satire;
and both as he interprets them are directed to a social
end. Lady Winchilsea's *A Pastoral Dialogue between Two
Shepherdesses* was printed in 1709 in the Sixth Part of the
Dryden–Tonson miscellany; and its inclusion there may
be significant, for Steele was on the editorial board making

the selections. It is described in the table as 'By the author of the Poem on the Spleen', which he had known and possibly had admired since 1701. *A Pastoral Dialogue* is conspicuously singled out in his brief review of the miscellany. In this volume notable for its pastoral poems he finds 'none superior' to it; and Lady Winchilsea's gentle satire and raillery are especially commended: 'all our little weaknesses' (Jenny Distaff spoke for Steele in the *Tatler* paper No. 10) 'are laid open in a manner more just and with truer raillery than ever man hit upon'. Its raillery also recommends Congreve's *Doris*. In *Spectator* No. 422, a paper analysing the types and the social usefulness of raillery, it is cited and quoted to the extent of several stanzas as 'a masterpiece of the best kind, when the satire is directed against vice with an air of contempt of the fault, but no ill-will to the criminal'. And likewise in the Dedication to Congreve of the *Poetical Miscellanies* Steele took another opportunity to praise 'my Favourite *Doris*' for this satirical quality:

... Your inimitable *Doris,* which excels, for Politeness, fine Raillery, and courtly Satyr, any Thing we can meet with in any Language. ... I cannot leave my Favourite *Doris,* without taking Notice how much that short Performance discovers a True Knowledge of Life. *Doris* is the Character of a Libertine Woman of Condition, and the Satyr is work'd up accordingly: For People of Quality are seldom touched with any Representation of their Vices, but in a Light which makes them Ridiculous.

Was this the kind of verse which in his mature years Steele himself aspired to write—the short poem marked by humour and delicate raillery, with an undercurrent of reproval? It is a temptation to apply such a criterion to anonymous verse strongly suspected to come from his pen, for example *To Belinda* and *On Nicolini's leaving the Stage.* No trace of a social purpose, however, is seen in the light love-song 'From Place to Place forlorn I go' written near the end of his career, and one may believe that a number of unacknowledged poems in this vein of Waller's simplicity and sweetness were scattered through the years. Apparently, moreover, there never was a time between 1701 and 1724 when the dashing off of a prologue or an epilogue did not fascinate him; but the friend who called him 'a veteran in this sort of composition' probably knew of pieces lost to us.

The reasons are obvious which made Steele deprive himself of the pleasures of dilettantism. Lack of self-confidence kept the young private from putting his name to *The Procession*, the first venture into print, which somehow he did find the courage to dedicate to the great soldier Lord Cutts. Then, even as a young man about town before settling down to a place in government service and eventually to the vocation of social reform and political pamphleteering, he was abashed at the triviality of his poetic themes of love and gallantry—'the gay Noise', 'the little Follies of the Fair', and 'Dames expiring with the Spleen'. And in a later period, awed by the poetical achievement of his gifted fellows, especially those who excelled in the short forms it was his aspiration to write, he concealed his versifying efforts in anonymity and afterwards ignored them. Only once in a while, usually in reference to a prologue or play-song, did he show any sign of the pleasurable satisfaction of the dilettante, for example in the comment on the prologue intended for the players at Hampton Court: 'I think this the best piece that Author has produced,' he said, 'as it frequently happens in matters which come from the heart.' And with a burst of outraged pride he continued: 'I shall insert this *little Poem*, for so Critick Dennis somewhere calls any thing shorter than five thousand six hundred and fifteen lines, including half lines, for speaking half sense, and broken passion—'.

At the height of his prestige as editor of the *Tatler*, *Spectator*, and *Guardian*, in the summer of 1713, his anthology *Poetical Miscellanies* was planned, a project no doubt conceived by the publisher Tonson. Several years had passed since the publication of the last volume of the Dryden–Tonson miscellany, and another collection was needed to meet competition with London booksellers. Tonson had found a good client in Steele, as the *Christian Hero* in several editions, two of the plays, the collected *Spectator*, and the original issues of the *Guardian* had demonstrated; Steele, on his side, probably agreed readily to be sponsor of the miscellany, and in the advertisement column of the *Guardian* on 4 May made the first announcement of the undertaking and invited contributions. The book was published on 29 December (*Englishman* No. 37) at the same time as the collected *Guardian*, and in the Dedication to Congreve he expressed satisfaction in the accomplishment:

I know, indeed, no Argument against these Collections, in Comparison of any other *Tonson* has heretofore Printed; but that there are in it no Verses of Yours:

Something of pride also underlies the phrase: 'the following Performances of my Self and Friends.' The 'friends', some of whose poems are plainly labelled, were Pope, George Jeffreys, Philips, and Lady Winchilsea—who head the list in that order—Parnell, Tickell, Gay, Budgell, Harrison, James Ward, Eusden, and Young. Conspicuously missing besides Congreve are Swift and Addison. The two signed poems by Steele are *The Procession. A Poem on the Funeral of Queen Mary, Written in the Year 1695* and *To Mr. Congreve, Occasion'd by his Comedy, call'd The Way of the World*. Of the eighty-five pieces included in the first edition about half are unassigned; and among the unassigned without any doubt at all are several of his own poems. The title of the volume and the facts of its publication are as follows: Poetical Miscellanies, Consisting of *Original Poems* and Translations. *By the best Hands*. Publish'd by Mr. *Steele*. For Jacob Tonson. 1714. 8vo. First edition misdated MDDCXIV. Second edition dated MDCCXIV. Third edition (called second) with additional pieces, 1727, 12mo. Pirated edition containing a small portion of the contents of the original printed by S. Powell for J. Thompson in Dublin, 1726, 8vo.

Three of the poems known to be Steele's appeared first as separate publications: *The Procession, Prologue to the University of Oxford,* and *Epilogue to the Town* (with Welsted's *Prologue*); and also a fourth, probably his, *Prologue at the Opening of the Theatre-Royal the Day after His Majesty's Publick Entry.* Two small pieces and a number of fragments are extant in autograph in the Blenheim MSS., and a prologue and an epilogue in holograph are preserved in a contemporary commonplace book; these remained unprinted until recent years, but everything else known to be his verse or thought to be was printed in his lifetime. Several pieces first appeared in early periodicals, Henry Playford's *Diverting Post* and John Oldmixon's *Muses Mercury,* and in three miscellanies of composite authorship at the turn of the century—Tom Brown's *Commendatory Verses* and volumes edited by Charles Gildon, *A New Collection of Poems* and *Examen Miscellaneum.* If the Sixth Part, 1709, of the Dryden–Tonson miscellany contains any specimens of his verse—and a reasonable supposition is that it does—they cannot be identified with certainty. Fewer than might be expected are scattered through the periodicals: the Martial epigrams he used in the *Tatler* and *Spectator,* and the prologues and one epilogue intended to be spoken on special occasions are printed in *Town-Talk* and the *Theatre.* The other prologues and epilogues spoken at first performances are found with the text of the plays, as of course are the incidental songs written for his own four plays. As is stated above, the *Poetical Miscellanies* contains both acknowledged and unacknowledged poems. Apparently he took little note, if any, of the reprinting of a number of the poems from time to time in such collections as Boyer's *Letters of Wit, Politicks, and Morality,* Fenton's *Oxford and Cambridge Miscellany Poems,* D'Urfey's *Wit and Mirth or Pills to Purge Melancholy,* Oldmixon's [?] *Bee,* John Walsh's *Monthly Masks of Vocal Musick,* where appeared several of the play-songs with their settings, and Tonson's *Odes and Satyrs of Horace.*

These then are the sources of Steele's poems in first and reprinted forms as they appeared in his lifetime. It may be thought strange that they are so few in number; but after persistent search nothing else from his pen can be identified in the early miscellanies, in the annals of Grub Street, or in the periodicals which accepted verse contributions from Motteux's *Gentleman's Journal*, 1692–4, to the *Monthly Miscellany or Memoirs for the Curious*, 1707–10. The results are also negative in a search through the dozens of miscellanies and octavo *Poems on Several Occasions* then in fashion published during the decades immediately preceding and immediately following his death, when his name was famous.

As the century wore on only the epigrams, prologues and epilogues, and songs—those small-verse genres of such great popularity with eighteenth-century readers— were reprinted; they appeared in special collections, the incidental play-songs particularly being frequently included in song books and miscellanies with or without their settings and as often as not anonymous. Steele is not represented in the repositories which preserved the verse not only of the talented poets of the century but the third-rate versifiers, whose very names are long since forgotten: his verse is not to be found in Dodsley's *Collection of Poems in Six Volumes by Several Hands*, 1748–58, 1765, or in Pearch's *Collection of Poems in Four Volumes by Several Hands, Intended as a Supplement to Mr. Dodsley's Collection*, 1770, 1783, or in *The Works of the Most Celebrated Minor Poets*, in three volumes, 1749–50, or in Davies's *Miscellaneous and Fugitive Pieces* in three volumes, 1773–4, or in Anderson's *Works of the British Poets*, in many volumes, 1795; there is nothing of course in the Johnson collections; and Steele had no 'lucky trifle' to find him a place in *The New Foundling Hospital for Wit*, 1784. In fact his name as versifier might have been entirely forgotten had it not been for John Nichols, his great editor and sincere admirer, who gave thought to the survival of his poetical efforts; in the anthology *A Select Collection of Poems With*

*Notes* in eight volumes, 1780–2, Nichols printed five pieces known to be from Steele's pen, and drawing heavily upon the *Poetical Miscellanies*, everything there that might possibly be his—but without specific attributions.

From first to last Steele's reputation as a poet has been slender, and of course deservedly so. As we know, early in the century young 'Captain Steele', the author of several successful plays, was an acceptable contributor to two or three anthologies; and in the years 1706 to 1708 there are a few complimentary references to his verse. Thomas Tickell in the poem *Oxford*, 1707, commended Codrington and Steele as warriors who wrote poetry in 'an easy, unaffected strain'; and a fellow Oxonian Thomas Bishop addressed *Captain S. on his Poetry* in the *Oxford and Cambridge Miscellany Poems*, 1708. In 1723 Giles Jacob listed him in the *Poetical Register* (ii. 207) with the cautious praise that his poetical writings, though few, deserved notice, because there 'is good Sense throughout, and some of the Wit natural to Sir Richard Steele'. The three mentioned there—Queen Mary's funeral poem, the Horatian ode applied to Marlborough, and the epistle to Congreve—were as likely as not submitted by Steele himself as poems which he considered dignified by subject and treatment and worthy of being remembered. At mid-century the editors of *Biographia Britannica* and of *The Lives of the Poets* did not bother even to bring up the question of his poetry, and in *Addisoniana*, 1803, the judgement was blunt: 'he had no genius for rhyme and he knew he had not, and therefore seldom attempted it' (ii. 242 ff.). It was John Nichols alone who kept the subject alive by favourable note and comment. By the end of the nineteenth century, however, the very titles were forgotten; and a group of Steele scholars, among them the biographers Dobson and Aitken, writing a series of articles on the subject for *Notes and Queries*, March to June 1885, found it difficult to form jointly even an incomplete list of his poems.

In this volume in which, whatever may be their merit,

they are for the first time all brought together, they are
arranged chronologically within homogeneous groups
according to the date of publication, in most cases the
only clue to the date of composition. The text used is that
first printed except for the few Steele revised, and for
these the alterations are indicated in footnotes. An introductory note for each outlines the occasion and the general
background and states the facts concerning its first appearance and later reprintings. Poems for which there is
no absolute proof of Steele's authorship are placed together
as tentative attributions. Of the nine pieces printed in this
group John Nichols hesitantly suggested three; the others
are for the first time assigned to Steele. In making these
attributions the present editor has considered the prob-
abilities in such external circumstances as the occasion,
the time and place of publication, and the similarity to his
acknowledged verse of the subject-matter, tone, and treatment, and the idiosyncrasies of diction and locution. One
of the problems of course has been the ruling out of other
possible authors. Then, quite apart from the tentative
attributions, and listed by title only, is a second group of
doubtful poems which it is thought well to mention as
having at least been considered as Steele's, on one ground
or another, but finally rejected for want of decisive evidence. The demonstrably incorrect attributions of the past
are listed and also those few pieces thought to exist of
which no trace has been found. The facts and assumptions
about all of these poems are set forth as fully as possible
in the annotations. Corrections and additions by readers
who have more knowledge than the present editor has of
minor and fugitive eighteenth-century verse are expected
and will be welcomed.

What can be assembled of Steele's verse is scant and
of little intrinsic value, and the collecting and annotating
of it would hardly be worth the effort expended were
Steele merely one of 'the mob of gentlemen' who wrote
with ease. But because of his achievement in other
fields, his verse-writing takes on something more than

antiquarian interest, and a brief study of it may possibly make a small contribution to literary history. It is the hope of the editor that Addison's definition of a critic will not be applicable to the reader of Steele's verse in this collection: 'A man who on all occasions is more attentive to what is wanting than what is present.'

# The Proceffion.

A

# P O E M

ON

# Her Majefties

# FUNERAL.

By a Gentleman of the Army.

*Munere* ———— ———— *Fungar inani* Virg.

*LONDON*,
Printed for *John Whitlock* in *Amen-Corner* near *Stationers-Hall*. 1695.

## The *Procession*. A Poem on the Funeral of Queen *Mary*. Written in the Year 1695. By Mr. *Steele*.

THE Days of Man are doom'd to Pain and Strife,
Quiet and Ease are *Foreign* to our Life;
No Satisfaction is, below, sincere,
Pleasure it self has something that's *severe*:
But long the fickle, wayward *British* Isle
Its Sorrows did with flattering Joys beguile;[1]
To Wild Excess their Frantick Humours flie,
While *WILLIAM's flowing* Fortunes buoy 'em high:
But a chill Damp, and Faintness seize on all,
By Dread *MARIA's Universal* Fall:
Their wonted[2] Luxury all Orders leave,
With[3] Joynt-consent to be their Selves, and *Grieve*.

From distant Homes the *Pitying Nations* come,
A *Mourning World* attends her to the Tomb:[4]
The Poor, Her First and Deepest Mourners are,
First in Her *Thoughts*, and Earliest in Her Care;
All Hand in Hand with common Friendly Woe,
In Poverty, our *Native* State, they go:
Some whom unstable Errors did engage,
By Luxury in Youth, to Need in Age:
Some who had Virgin Vows for Wedlock broke,
And where, they Help expected, found a *Yoke*;
Others who in their Want, feel double Weight
From the Remembrance of a *Plenteous* State;[5]

[1] Did with *false* Mirth and Joy it self beguile;
[2] usual
[3] *Misprinted* Will *1714*
[4] A *Mourning World* t' attend her to her Tomb:
[5] *Couplet ending here*: Others who labour with the double Weight
Of Want, and Mem'ry of a *Plenteous* State;

There Mothers walk, who oft[6] despairing stood,
Pierc'd with their Infants deafning Sobs for Food;
Then to a Dagger ran, with threat'ning Eyes
To stab their Bosoms, and to hush their Cries;
But in the thought they stopp'd, their Locks they tore,
Threw down the Steel, and *Cruelly* forbore:[7]
The Innocents their Parent's Love *forgive*,
Smile at their Fate, nor know they are to *live*:
These modest Wants had ne'er been understood,
But by MARIA's *Cunning* to be good;
None on their State now cast a Pitying Eye,
Hear their Complaints, or will their Want supply;
They move as if they went, (so deep's their Moan)
Not only to Her Grave, but to their own;
That were Relief, but coming Days they mourn,
Oppress'd with Life, and *fearful* to *return*.

With *Dread* Concern, the *Awful* Senate came,
Their *Grief*, as all their Passions, is the *same*.

The next Assembly dissipates our Fears,
The *Stately Mourning* Throng of *British* Peers;
There, is each Member skill'd, and able known
For ev'ry weighty Purpose of a Throne;
T' adorn, or to defend their Native Isle,
Or Jarring Neighbour States to reconcile;
But most from *Ormond's* Port our Souls we chear,
And Hecatombs expect for every Tear:
For to the Foe is certain Vengeance sent,
When Heroes *suffer*, and the Brave *lament*;
To one their every Character may fall,
*Sommers*, th' accomplish'd Tongue which speaks 'em all,[8]
That *comprehensive* Man unskill'd in naught,
With all the Arts of Learn'd Assemblies fraught;
Ready his Wit, his Language Free and *Pure*,
His Judgment Quick and Sudden, yet *mature*;

6 who oft] wh' have oft        7 *Misprinted* forbear *1714*
8 Sommer's, th' implicit Man that speaks 'em all,

He can their different Powers at once dispense,
So justly is he form'd to *speak their Sense*:
But now dumb Sorrow represents 'em more,
Than e'er his Powerful Eloquence before,
Though when his Lips with their known Sweetness⁹
 flow,
The *World 's as silent*, as himself is now.

Now all are Past, yon' Wond'rous Man appears,
We yield to *Gay Distress* and comely Tears:
*Villars*! A Name design'd by Nature Chief,
T' invite to Joy, or reconcile to *Grief*.
The Gross of Men were to course Uses Born,
But Heav'n made them Creation to *adorn*;
With mix'd disturb'd Delight by all is seen,
His *Moving* Manner, and his *Speaking* Mien;
Rage, Pity, and Disdain at once we trace,
In the *distracted* Beauties of his Face;
We measure his each Step, each Motion scan,
The *Grief* of Woman! but the *Strength* of Man!
To such an Height his swoln Afflictions grow,
H' inspires the Steed he leads with Human¹⁰ Woe;
The *Generous* Beast looks back to 's Purple Side,
And now *laments*, what was before his *Pride*:
No more at Voice of Martial¹¹ Musick bounds,
He feels *New Passions*¹² as the Trumpet sounds;
Nor knows what Power his Courage stole away,
But heaves into big *Sighs* when he would *Neigh*.
Here at a stand our weary'd Sorrow seems,
Rack'd with new Forms, and tortur'd with Extremes
E'er this sad Triumph past we found Relief,
Continu'd Anguish lost the sense of Grief;
But still the Chariot fainting Force supply'd,
Anew we all reviv'd, anew we dy'd;
Grief did all bounds ambitiously deny,
Swell'd every Breast, and melted every Eye.

9 Rhet'rick          10 Humane
11 Warring          12 Passion

Lo! Death himself! See him Triumphant ride!
Lo! the *Grim Being* moves with sullen Pride;
His Jaws are glutted for th' ensuing Year,
He'll shun our Cities, and our Armies *spare*:
The Mourners[13] plac'd on high with Looks deject,
With down intended Looks our Souls direct.
Gold, Purple, Tissue, *Crowns*, *Enchant* the sight,
And move our Grief, that us'd to give *Delight*.
There drowsie Gems their Nature know no more,
But gather *Darkness* now, as *Light* before;
There all that's Bright i' th' *Widow'd* World is seen,
Too faint t' express, ev'n the *Departed Queen*.

No Mortal Beauty yet recalls an Eye,
The next bright Objects[14] pass neglected by;
But as the Fair ones[15] March, the lengthening Row
Inspires a more familiar *Kindly Woe*:[16]
One Universal Face their Passion wears,
But *Darby* hides in vain her *Gushing Tears*,[17]
In Her Affliction takes an abject State,
Something so very[18] *Low*, yet very *Great*;
No single Cause so *different* Grief cou'd send,
She Weeps as *Subject*, *Servant*, and a *Friend*:
To close the Pomp, the Fair Attendant Maids
Appear *true Angels* dress'd like *fancy'd Shades*;[19]
Their clouded *Beauties* speak Man's *gawdy* Strife,
The glittering Miseries of Humane Life.

Who that these passing Obsequies had seen,
Wou'd e'er believe this were that *very Queen*;

---

[13] Ladies
[14] next bright Objects] nearest Mourners
[15] Fair ones] Ladies
[16] *omitted couplet here*] Sure that's the Region of departed Loves,
          Such *Gloomy Day* enlights th' Elysian Groves;
[17] But *Darby's smother'd* Sighs and *Gushing* Tears,
[18] humbly
[19] *omitted couplet here*] Their Grief imparts t' unpitied Lover's ease,
          Sadly they Charm, and *dismally* they Please:

That very Queen, whom Heav'n so lately gave
A *Crown*, in the same Place where, now, a *Grave*!
I see Her yet, Nature and Fortune's Pride,
A *Scepter* Grac'd her Hand, a *King* her Side,
Cœlestial Youth and Beauty did impart
Extatick[20] Vision to the coldest Heart:
We saw her Children should succeed her sway,
And *future Monarchs* round her Table Play.
Her People's Acclamations rend the Skies,
The ecchoing Firmament returns their Cries.
She unconcern'd and careless all the while,
Rewards their loud Applauses with a *Smile*,
With easie Majesty, and *Humble State*,
Smiles at the *trifle Power*, and knows its date.
What being prov'd so furiously enclin'd,
For Power each Morn *assum'd*,[21] each Night *resign'd*?
So short a Period to Her Glories giv'n,
The *Crime* of Fate, and the Reproach of Heav'n!

But to the sacred Fane the Pomp is led,[22]
The Wide *Capacious Palace* of the Dead.[23]
What Hands commit the Beauteous, Good and Just,
The Dearer Part of *WILLIAM* to the Dust?
In Her his Vital Heat, his Glory lies,
In Her the Monarch liv'd, in Her he Dies.
One was their Soul:[24] while he secur'd Her Rest,
War's Hardships seem'd Luxurious to his Breast:
And he Abroad, no Peace Repose could yield;
She felt the distant *Dangers* of the Field.
No form of State makes the Great Man forego,
The Task due to *Her Love*, and to *His Woe*;

[20] Prophetick
[21] For Power each Morn *assum'd*,] For that Sh' *each day assum'd*,
[22] But now the Pomp to th' sacred Abbey's led,
[23] *two omitted couplets here*] The Glaring Lamps disturb their *usual Night*,
        They half awaken'd with th' intruding Light.
        Souls to a *Slumber* Wake, and move their Clay,
        They think her Pile, their *Resurrection* Day.
[24] Soul:] Soul

Since his kind Frame can't the large Suffering bear,
In Pity to his People, he's not here:
For to the mighty Loss we now receive,
The next Affliction were to see him *Grieve*.[25]

*FINIS.*

[25] *three omitted couplets here*]

> There, MARY, undisturb'd in quiet Sleep,
> None shall Profane the Urn thy Ashes keep,
> Till, time's no more, by all thou shalt be read,
> And be a Monument to thy Neighbour dead;
> For *British* Bards thy Memory shall save,
> And snatch thy Eternal Virtue from the Grave.

*FINIS.*

# EPISTLES AND POEMS
## OF COMPLIMENT

*To the Mirrour of British Knighthood, the
Worthy Author of the* Satyr against Wit;
*Occasion'd by the Hemystick,* P. 8.—
Heav'ns Guard poor *A——n.*

Must I then passive stand! and can I hear
The Man I Love, abus'd, and yet forbear?
Yet much I thank thy Favour to my Friend,
'Twas some Remorse thou didst not him commend.
Thou dost not all my Indignation raise,
For I prefer thy Pity to thy Praise;

In vain thou woud'st thy Name, dull Pedant, hide,
There's not a Line but smells of thy *Cheapside,*
If *Caesar's* Bounty for your Trash you've shar'd,
You're not the first Assassine he has spar'd.
His Mercy, not his Justice, made thee Knight.
Which *P—rt—r* may demand with equal Right.

Well may'st thou think an useless Talent Wit,
Thou who without it hast three Poems Writ:
Impenetrably dull, secure thou'rt found,
And can'st receive no more, than give a Wound;
Then, scorn'd by all, to some dark Corner fly,
And in Lethargic Trance expiring lie,
Till thou from injur'd *G—rth* thy Cure receive,
And *S——d* only Absolution give.

# To Mr. *Congreve, Occasion'd by his Comedy,* *call'd,* The Way of the World. By Mr. *Steele.*[1]

WHEN Pleasure's falling[2] to the low Delight,
In the vain Joys of the uncertain Sight,
No Sense of Wit when rude Spectators know,
But in distorted Gesture, Farce and Show,
How could, great Author,[3] your[4] aspiring Mind
Dare to write only to the Few refin'd!
Yet tho' that nice Ambition you pursue,
'Tis not in *Congreve*'s Power to please but few.
Implicitly devoted to his Fame,
Well-dress'd Barbarians know his awful Name;
Tho' senseless they're of Mirth, but when they laugh,
As they feel[5] Wine, but when, 'till Drunk, they quaff.[6]
  On you, from Fate, a lavish Portion fell
In ev'ry way of Writing to excell.[7]
Your Muse Applause to *Arabella* brings,
In Notes as sweet as *Arabella* sings,
When e'er you draw[8] an undissembled Woe,
With sweet Distress your Rural Numbers flow;
*Pastora*'s the Complaint of ev'ry Swain,
*Pastora* still the Eccho of the Plain!
Or if your Muse describe, with warming Force,
The wounded *Frenchman* falling from his Horse;

---

[1] Epistle to Mr. Congreve . . . By Mr. Steele. 01 G: To Mr. Congreve . . .
By Captain Steel. 01 B
[2] When pleasure is fallen 01 G: When Pleasure is fall'n 01 B
[3] great Author,] great Congreve, 01 B
[4] thy 01 G, 01 B (*nine similar alterations made 1710*)
[5] fill 01 B (*misprint?*)
[6] *At this point four lines included* 01 G, 01 B
           Forgotten Author's, who have lately Writ,
           Despair now to revive their fame of Wit;
           Hard fate, that all Poetick hopes are fled,
           Spite of that help to Glory being Dead;
[7] *Couplet following omitted* 01 B           [8] sigh 01 G: sing 01 B

And her own *William* glorious in the Strife,
Bestowing on the prostrate Foe his Life:
You the great Act[9] as gen'rously Rehearse,
And all the English Fury's in[10] your Verse.
By your selected[11] Scenes, and handsome[12] Choice,
Ennobled Comedy exalts her Voice;
You check unjust Esteem and fond Desire,
And teach to Scorn, what[13] else we should Admire;
The just Impression taught by you we bear,[14]
The Player acts the World, the World the Player,
Whom still that[15] World unjustly disesteems,
Tho'[16] he, alone, professes what he seems:
But when your Muse assumes her Tragick Part,
She conquers and she reigns in ev'ry Heart;
To mourn[17] with her, Men cheat their private Woe,
And gen'rous Pity's all the Grief they know;
The Widow, who impatient of Delay,
From the Town-joys must Mask it to the Play,
Joins with your *Mourning-Bride's* resistless Moan,
And weeps a Loss she slighted, when her own;
You give us Torment, and you give us Ease,
And vary our Affections[18] as you please;
Is not a Heart so kind as yours in Pain,
To load your Friends with Cares[19] you only feign;[20]
Your friends in Grief, compos'd yourself, to leave?
But 'tis the only way you'll e'er deceive.
Then still, great Sir,[21] your moving Pow'r employ,
To lull our Sorrow, and correct our Joy.

---

9 Deed o1 B
10 And all the *English* Fury's in] And all the *English* fire is in o1 G, o1 B
11 politer o1 B          12 juster o1 B                13 where o1 G, o1 B
14 hear o1 G (*misprint?*)      15 the o1 G      16 For o1 B      17 moan o1 B
18 Afflictions o1 G, *1710* (*misprint?*)
19 Care o1 G
20 *Couplet following omitted* o1 B
21 Then still, great Sir,] But no, go on— o1 B

## To
## My Lov'd Tutour D.$^r$ Ellis

WITH Secret impulse thus do Streams return
To that Capacious Ocean whence they're born:
Oh Would but Fortune come w$^{th}$ bounty fraught
Proportion'd to y$^e$ mind w$^{ch}$ thou hast taught!

Till then let these unpolish'd Leaves impart
The Humble Offering of a Gratefull Heart.

Rich.$^d$ Steele

## An Imitation of the Sixth Ode of *Horace*, beginning, *Scriberis Vario fortis*. Apply'd to his Grace the Duke of Marlborough.

### Suppos'd to be made by Capt. R. S.

SHOU'D Addison's Immortal Verse,
Thy Fame in Arms, great Prince, Rehearse,
With Anna's Lightning you'd appear,
And glitter o'er again in War:
Repeat the Proud Bavarian's Fall!
And in the Danube plunge the Gaul!

'Tis not for me thy Worth to show,
Or Lead Achilles to the Foe;
Describe stern Diomed in Fight,
And put the wounded Gods to Flight:
I dare not, with unequal Rage,
On such a Mighty Theam ingage;
Nor Sully in a Verse like mine,
Illustrious Anna's Praise, and Thine.

Let the laborious Epic strain
In lofty numbers sing the Man,
That bears to distant Worlds his Arms,
And frights the German with Alarms:
His Courage and his conduct tell,
And on his various Virtues dwell.
In trifling Cares my humble Muse
A less Ambitious Tract pursues,
Instead of Troops in Battel mixt,
And Gauls with British Spears transfixt:
She Paints the soft Distress and Mein
Of Dames expiring with the Spleen.

From the gay Noise affected Air,
And little Follies of the Fair,
A slender stock of Fame I raise,
And draw from others Faults, my Praise.

# Verses to the Author of the Tragedy of *Cato*.

WHILE you the Fierce divided Britons awe,
And Cato, with an equal Virtue, draw,
While Envy is it self in Wonder lost,
And Factions strive who shall applaud you most;
Forgive the fond Ambition of a Friend,
Who hopes himself, not you to recommend;
And joins th' Applause which all the Learn'd bestow
On one, to whom a perfect Work they owe.
To my* light Scenes I once inscrib'd your Name,
And impotently strove to borrow Fame:
Soon will that die, which adds thy Name to mine,
Let me, then, live, join'd to a Work of thine.

Richard Steele

* Tender Husband, *Dedicated to Mr.* Addison. [*Note in* Cato]

# THE
# SONGS IN THE PLAYS

## *The Funeral*

Let not Love on me bestow
Soft Distress, and tender Woe;
I know none but substantial Blisses,
Eager Glances, solid Kisses;
I know not what the Lovers feign,
Of finer Pleasure mix'd with Pain;
Then prethee give me gentle Boy,
None of thy Grief but all thy Joy.

### Boy *Sings.*

**I.**

Ye Minutes bring the happy Hour,
And *Chloe* Blushing to the Bower:
Then shall all Idle Flames be o're,
Nor Eyes or Heart e're wander more:
Both, *Chloe*, fix'd for e're on Thee,
For Thou art all thy Sex to Me.

**II.**

A Guilty is a false Embrace,
*Corinna's* Love's a Fairy-Chace:
Begone, thou Meteor, Fleeting Fire,
And all, that can't survive Desire.
*Chloe* my Reason moves and Awe,
And *Cupid* shot Me, when he Saw.

**I.**

*Cynderaxa* Kind and Good,
Has all my Heart and Stomach too;
She makes me love, not hate, my Food,
As other peevish Wenches do.

### II.

When *Venus* leaves her *Vulcan's* Cell,
Which all but I a Cole-hole call;
Fly, fly yee that above Stairs dwell,
Her Face is wash'd, yee vanish all.

### III.

And as she's Fair, she can impart
That Beauty, to make all things Fine;
Brightens the Floor with Wondrous Art,
And at her touch the Dishes shine.

## Set by Mr. *Daniel Purcell.*

## Sung by *Jemmie Bowin.*

### I.

On Yonder Bed supinely laid,
Behold thy Lov'd Expecting Maid:
In Tremor, Blushes, half in Tears,
Much, much she Wishes, more she fears.
Take, take her to thy Faithful Arms
Hymen bestows thee all her Charms.

### II.

Heav'n to thee Bequeaths the Fair
To raise thy Joy, and lull thy Care;
Heav'n made Grief, if Mutual, cease,
But Joy, divided, to encrease;
To Mourn with her exceeds delight,
Darkness with her, the Joys of Light.

## Sung by Mr. *Pate.*

### I.

Arise, arise great Dead for Arms renown'd,
Rise from your Urns, and save your Dying story,
Your Deeds will be in Dark Oblivion Drown'd
For Mighty *William* Seizes all your Glory.

II.

Again the *British* Trumpet Sounds,
Again *Britannia* Bleeds;
To Glorious Death, or comely Wounds,
Her Godlike Monarch Leads.

III.

Pay us, kind Fate, the Debt you Owe,
Celestial Minds from Clay untye;
Let Coward Spirits dwell below,
And only give the Brave to Die.

## *The Lying Lover*

### To *Celia's* Spinet.

Thou soft Machine that do'st her Hand obey,
Tell her my Grief in thy harmonious Lay.

To shun my Moan to thee she'll fly,
To her Touch be sure reply,
And, if she removes it, die.

Know thy Bliss, with Rapture shake,
Tremble o'er all thy numerous Make;
Speak in melting Sounds my Tears,
Speak my Joys, my Hopes, my Fears.

Thus force her when from me she'd fly,
By her own hand, like me, to die.

### Song, [sung] by Mr. *Leveridge*.

I.

*Venus* has left her Grecian Isles,
With all her gaudy Train
Of little Loves, soft Cares and Smiles,
In my larger Breast to reign.

2.

Ye tender Herds, and list'ning Deer,
Forget your Food, forget your Fear,
The bright *Victoria* will be here.

3.

The Savages about me throng,
Mov'd with the Passion of my Song,
And think *Victoria* stays too long.

Enter *Bookwit* with Bottle and Glass singing.

Since the Day of poor Man,
That little little Span,
Tho' long it can't last,
For the future, and past
Is spent with Remorse and Despair.
With such a full Glass
Let that of Life pass,
'Tis made up of Trouble,
A Storm tho' a Bubble,
There's no Bliss but forgetting your Care.

## Song.

### [Sung] By Mr. *Leveridge*.

1.

The rolling Years the Joys restore,
Which happy happy *Britain* knew,
When in a Female Age before
Beauty the Sword of Justice drew.

2.

Nymphs, and Fauns, and Rural Powers
Of christal Floods, and shady Bowers,
No more shall here preside:
The flowing Wave, and living Green
Owe only to their present Queen
Their Safety and their Pride.

3.

United Air, and Pleasures bring,
Of tender Note, and tuneful String:
All your Arts devoted are
To move the Innocent and Fair;
While they receive the pleasing Wound,
Eccho repeats the dying Sound.

## The Tender Husband

### A SONG.

### Design'd for the Fourth Act, but not Set.

I.

SEE, *Britons*, see with Awful Eyes,
  *Britannia* from her Seas arise!
Ten Thousand Billows round Me roar,
  While Winds and Waves engage,
That break in Froth upon my Shoar,
  And impotently Rage.
Such were the Terrors, which of late
  Surrounded my afflicted State;
United Fury thus was bent
  On my Devoted Seats,
'Till all the Mighty Force was spent
  In Feeble Swells, and Empty Threats.

II.

But now with rising Glory Crown'd,
My Joys run high, they know no Bound;
  Tides of unruly Pleasure flow
  Through ev'ry Swelling Vein;
  New Raptures in my Bosom glow,
And warm me up to Youth again.
  Passing Pomps my Streets Adorn;
  Captive Spoils, in Triumph born,

Standards of *Gauls*, in Fight subdu'd,
Colours in Hostile Blood embru'd,
   Ensigns of Tyrannic Might,
   Foes to Equity and Right,
In Courts of *British* Justice wave on high,
   Sacred to Law, and Liberty.
My Crowded Theatres repeat,
In Songs of Triumph, the Defeat.
   Did ever Joyful Mother see
   So Bright, so Brave a Progeny!
Daughters with so much Beauty Crown'd,
Or Sons for Valour so renown'd!


### III.

But oh I gaze, and seek in vain
To find amidst this Warlike Train
   My Absent Sons, that us'd to Grace
With decent Pride this Joyous Place:
Unhappy Youths! how do my Sorrows rise,
Swell my Breast, and melt my Eyes,
While I your mighty Loss deplore?
Wild, and raging with Distress,
I mourn, I mourn my own Success,
And boast my Victories no more.
Unhappy Youths! far from their native Sky,
   On *Danube's* Banks enterr'd they lye.
*Germania*, give me back my Slain,
   Give me my slaughter'd Sons again.
Was it for this they rang'd so far,
   To free thee from oppressive War?
        *Germania, &c.*


### IV.

Tears of Sorrow which I shed
O'er the Manes of my Dead,
Lasting Altars let me raise
To my living Heroes Praise;

Heav'n give them a longer Stay
　As Glorious Actions to Display,
　Or perish on as Great a Day.

### SONG.

WITH Studied Airs, and practis'd Smiles,
*Flavia* my Ravish'd Heart beguiles,
The Charms we make, are Ours alone,
Nature's works are not our own;
Her Skilful Hand gives every Grace,
And shows her fancy in her Face.
She Feeds with Art an Amourous Rage,
Nor fears the Force of Coming Age.

### A SONG.

#### 1.

WHY lovely Charmer, tell me why,
So very kind, and yet so shy?
Why does that cold forbidding Air
Give Damps of Sorrow and Despair?
Or why that Smile my Soul subdue,
And kindle up my Flames anew?

#### 2.

In vain you strive with all your Art,
By turns to freeze and fire my Heart:
When I behold a Face so fair,
So sweet a Look, so soft an Air,
My ravish'd Soul is charm'd all o'er,
I cannot love thee less nor more.

## A Sonnet! pray repeat it.

### 1.

WHILE Gentle *Parthenissa* walks,
And sweetly smiles, and gayly talks,
A thousand Shafts around her fly,
A thousand Swains unheeded die.

### 2.

If then she labours to be seen,
With all her killing Air and Mien;
From so much Beauty, so much Art,
What Mortal can secure his Heart?

## The Conscious Lovers

### 1.[1]

FROM Place to Place forlorn I go,
    With downcast Eyes a silent Shade;
Forbidden to declare my Woe;
    To speak, till spoken to, afraid.

### II.

My inward Pangs, my secret Grief,[2]
    My soft consenting Looks betray:[3]
He loves, but gives me no Relief:
    Why speaks not he who may?

[1] First printed in *The Theatre* No. 18, 1 March 1720, with the heading:
    The Love-sick Maid / A Song. Set by Mr. *Galliard*.
[2] Me to the Youth, who caus'd my Grief, *1720*
[3] My too consenting Looks betray: *1720*

# Indiana's SONG in the Conscious Lovers.

*From place to place forlorn I go, with down cast Eyes,*
*down cast Eyes, down cast Eyes a silent shade. Forbiden to de-*
*= clare, declare my woe, to speak, to speak till spoken to afraid.*

*My inward Pangs, my secret greif.*
*My soft consenting looks betray:*
*He Loves but gives me no releif.*
*Why speaks not he who may.*

Flute

*Engrav'd by J. Crofs*

# SHORT POEMS
# EPIGRAMS
## &c.

6.ᵈ

# THE
# Muses Mercury:
## OR,
# Monthly Miscellany.

### Consisting of
Poems, Prologues, Songs, Sonnets, Translations,
and other Curious Pieces, Never before Printed.

BY

The Earl of *Roscommon*,  } { Mr. *DENNIS*,
Mr. *DRYDEN*,  } { Dr. *N——n*,
Dr. *G——th*,  } { Capt. *STEEL*,
*N. TATE*, Esquire.  } { Mr. *MANNING*, &c.

To which is added,
An Account of the *STAGE*, of the New *OPERA'S* and
*PLAYS* that have been Acted, or are to be Acted this Season;
And of the New Books relating to *Poesy*, *Criticism*, &c. lately Publish'd.

For the Month of *FEBRUARY*.

#### To be continued Monthly.

SUA LAUREA PHŒBO

*Ex Quovis Ligno non fit Mercurius.*

*LONDON*, Printed by *J. H.* for Andrew Bell, at the *Cross Keys*
and *Bible* in *Cornhill*, near *Stocks-Market*. 1707.

18. March

*Verses on Mrs. Selwyn, Being Valentine.*

Upon having Mrs. Selwyn, by Lot, my Valentine.

ONE Minute, Fortune, Thou hast let me Live,
I freely all my Life, before, forgive.
Cares did, till now, my rising blisse destroy
And streaks of Sorrow ran through all my Joy.
But, Fickle Goddesse,[1] Thou art now sincere:
Quite happy now[2] I feel not hope, or fear;
Thy Wealth and Empire on thy slaves bestow,
Slaves[3] who no blisse, but Wealth and Empire know.
Be all thy Power in one great gift display'd,
And to these Arms convey the Lovely Maid;
I never will beseech thy bounty more,
But be as rough, and Angry as before.

[1] But now, fickle Goddesse: *cancelled*
[2] now *inserted above the line*        [3] Thy Slaves: *first written*

# To a Young Lady who had Marry'd an Old Man.

## By Capt. *Steel.*

### 1.

SINCE *Cælia* cou'd, to Love unjust,
Debauch'd by Wealth and Golden Charms[1]
Return before her Death to Dust
In hoary *Nestor's* feeble Arms.

### 2.

While Midnight Bowls my Passion break,
And no Intruding Cares molest;
Her may her Grisly Bridegroom wake,
And to no Joy disturb her rest.

[1] *Misprinted* Beauties Charms. *Corrected in the* errata *of the February issue, p.* 52

3.

Still while she glows with Youth and Fire,
May baffled Fondness teaze her Rage;
May he with hot, yet num'd Desire,
Burn like Youth, yet freeze like Age.


## Song. By Capt. *Steel.*

Me Cupid made a Happy Slave,
A merry wretched Man,
I slight the Nymphs I cannot have,
Nor Doat on those I can.

This constant Maxim still I hold,
To baffle all Despair;
The Absent Ugly are and Old,
The Present Young and Fair.


## Epigrams adapted from Martial.

### *Lib.* 1. *Ep.* 13.

Casta suo gladium cum traderet Arria Paeto,
    quem de visceribus strinxerat ipsa suis,
'Si qua fides, vulnus quod feci non dolet', inquit,
    'sed tu quod facies, hoc mihi, Paete, dolet.'

When Arria pull'd the Dagger from her Side,
Thus to her Consort spoke th' illustrious Bride:
The Wound I gave my self I do not grieve,
I die by that which Paetus must receive.

### De Vetula

TACTA places, audita places: si non videare,
    tota places: neutro, si videare, places.

WHILST in the Dark on thy soft Hand I hung
And heard the tempting Syren in thy Tongue,
What Flames, what Darts, what Anguish I endur'd?
But when the Candle enter'd I was cur'd.

### Lib. 1. Ep. 68.

QUIDQUID agit Rufus, nihil est nisi Naevia Rufo.
    si gaudet, si flet, si tacet, hanc loquitur.
cenat, propinat, poscit, negat, innuit: una est
    Naevia; si non sit Naevia, mutus erit.
scriberet hesterna patri cum luce salutem,
    'Naevia lux,' inquit, 'Naevia, lumen, have.'

LET Rufus weep, rejoice, stand, sit, or walk,
Still he can nothing but of Naevia talk.
Let him eat, drink, ask questions, or dispute,
Still he must speak of Naevia, or be mute.
He writ to his father, ending with this line,
I am, my lovely Naevia, ever thine.

### Lib. 4. Ep. 22.

PRIMOS passa toros et adhuc placanda marito
    merserat in nitidos se Cleopatra lacus,
dum fugit amplexus. sed prodidit unda latentem;
    lucebat, totis cum tegeretur aquis.
condita sic puro numerantur lilia vitro,
    sic prohibet tenues gemma latere rosas.
insilui mersusque vadis luctantia carpsi
    basia : perspicuae plus vetuistis aquae.

WHEN my bright Consort, now nor Wife nor Maid,⎫
Asham'd and wanton, of Embrace afraid,     ⎬
Fled to the Streams, the Streams my Fair betray'd. ⎭
To my fond Eyes she all transparent stood,
She blushed, I smil'd at the slight covering Flood.
Thus through the Glass the lovely Lilly glows,
Thus through the ambient Gem shines forth the Rose.
I saw new Charms, and plung'd to seize my Store,
Kisses I snatch'd, the Waves prevented more.

## Toasts for the Kit-Cat Club.

BRIGHT dames when first we meet unheeded passe
We read frail charms on Monuments of Glasse.

In Joylesse Streams the Purple Chrystall flows
Till each is nam'd for whome each Bosom glows.

Then Friendship Love and Wine Unite their fires
Then all their Homage pay, where each admires.

## Song.

By what Power did she enslave me!
Pretty Maid, the Kiss she gave me!
On her Lips the Ruby glow'd,
And the Breath of Violets blow'd;
Swell'd with moist and balmy Heat;
All was Honey, melting sweet:
Boundless Joys e'en now I prove,
For I drank a World of Love:
Wanton, madding with the Bliss,
Still I taste the charming Kiss.

# PROLOGUES
### AND
# EPILOGUES

## The Funeral

## PROLOGUE,

### Spoken by Mr. *Wilks*.

NATURE's Deserted and Dramatick Art,
To Dazle now the Eye, has left the Heart;
Gay Lights, and Dresses, long extended Scenes,
Dæmons and Angels moving in Machines,
All that can now or please or fright the Fair⎫
May be perform'd without a writer's Care,　⎬
And is the Skill of Carpenter, not Player:　⎭
Old *Shakespear's* Days could not thus far Advance,
But what's his Buskin to our Ladder Dance?
In the mid Region a silk Youth to stand,
With that unweildy Engine at Command!
Gorg'd with intemp'rate Meals while here you sit,
Well may you take Activity for Wit:
Fie, Let confusion on such Dulness seize.
Blush you're so Pleas'd, as we that so we Please;
But we still kind to your inverted Sence,
Do most unnatural Things once more dispense;
For since You're still prepost'rous in Delight,⎫
Our Author made, a full House to invite,　⎬
A Funeral a Comedy to night.　　　　⎭
Nor does he fear that you will take the Hint,
And let the Funeral his own be meant;
No, in Old *England* nothing can be won
Without a Faction Good or Ill be done;
To own this our Frank Author does not fear,
But Hopes for a prevailing Party here,
He knows h' has num'rous Friends, nay knows they'll
　show it,
And for the Fellow-Soldier save the Poet,

## *The Funeral*

### EPILOGUE,

#### Spoken by Lord *Hardy*.

LOVE, Hope and Fear, Desire, Aversion, Rage,⎱
All that can move the Soul, or can asswage, ⎰
Are drawn in Miniature of Life the stage. ⎰
Here you can view your Selves, and here is shown
To what you're born in Sufferings not your own.
The Stage to Wisdom's no Fantastick Way,
*Athens* her self learn't Virtue at a Play.
Our Author me to-Night a Souldier drew:
But faintly Writ, what warmly you pursue:
To his great purpose, had he Equal Fire,
He'd not aim to please only, but inspire;
He'd sing what hovering Fate attends our Isle,
And from base Pleasure rouse to glorious Toil:
Full time the Earth to a new Decision brings;
While *William* gives the *Roman* Eagle Wings:
With Arts and Arms shall *Brittain* Tamely end,
Which naked Picts so bravely could Defend?
The Painted Heroes on th' Invaders press,
And think their Wounds Addition to their Dress;
In Younger Years we've been with Conquest Blest,
And Paris has the *Brittish* Yoke confess'd;
Is't then in *England*, in lost *England* known,
Her King's are nam'd from a Revolted Throne?
But we offend—You no Examples need,
In Imitation of your selves proceed;
'Tis you your Countries Honour must secure,
Be all your Actions Worthy of *Namur*:
With Gentle Fires your Gallantry improve,
Courage is Brutal if untouch'd with Love:

If soon our utmost Bravery's not display'd,
Think that Right[1] Circle must be Captives made.
Let Thoughts of saving them our Toils beguile,
And they Reward our Labours with a Smile.

## *The Lying Lover*
### PROLOGUE.

ALL the commanding Powers that awe Mankind
Are in a trembling Poet's Audience join'd,
Where such bright Gallaxies of Beauty sit,
And at their Feet assembled Men of Wit;
Our Author therefore owns his deep Despair
To entertain the Learned or the Fair:
Yet hopes that both will so much be his Friends,
To pardon what he does, for what h' intends;
He aims to make the coming Action move
On the dread Laws of Friendship, and of Love:
Sure then he'll find but very few severe,
Since there's of both so many Objects here;
He offers no gross Vices to your Sight,
Those too much Horrour raise for just Delight,
And to detain th' attentive knowing Ear,
Pleasure must still have something that's severe;
If then you find our Author treads the Stage
With just Regard to a reforming Age;
He hopes, he humbly hopes, you'll think there's due
Mercy to him, for Justice done to you.

## *The Lying Lover*
### EPILOGUE.

OUR too advent'rous Author soar'd to Night
Above the little Praise, Mirth to excite,
And chose with Pity to chastise Delight.

[1] *? Misprint for* Bright

For Laughter's a distorted Passion, born
Of sudden self Esteem, and sudden Scorn;
Which, when 'tis o'er, the Men in Pleasure wise,
Both him that mov'd it, and themselves despise;
While generous Pity of a painted Woe
Make us our selves both more approve, and know.
What is that Touch within, which Nature gave
For Man to Man, e'er Fortune made a Slave?
Sure it descends from that dread Power alone,
Who levels Thunder from His awful Throne,
And shakes both Worlds,—yet hears the wretched Groan.

'Tis what the antient Sage could ne'er define,
Wonder'd—and call'd, part human, part divine:
'Tis that pure Joy, which guardian Angels know,
When timely they assist their Care below,
When they the good protect, the ill oppose,
'Tis what our Sovereign feels, when she bestows,
Which gives her glorious Cause such high Success,
That only on the Stage you see Distress.


## The Tender Husband

### EPILOGUE,

#### Spoken by Mr. *Eastcourt*.

*BRITONS*, who constant War, with factious Rage,
For Liberty against each other wage,
From Foreign Insult save this *English* Stage.
No more th' *Italian* squaling Tribe admit,
In Tongues unknown; 'tis Popery in Wit.
The Songs (their selves confess) from *Rome* they bring;
And 'tis High-Mass, for ought you know, they Sing.
Husbands take Care, the Danger may come nigher,
The Women say their Eunuch is a Friar.

But is it not a serious Ill to see
*Europe*'s great Arbiters so mean can be;
Passive, with an affected Joy to sit,
Suspend their native Taste of Manly Wit;
Neglect their Comic Humour, Tragic Rage,
For known Defects of Nature, and of Age.
Arise for shame, ye Conqu'ring *Britons* rise,
Such unadorn'd Effeminacy despise;
Admire (if you will doat on Foreign Wit)
Not what *Italians* Sing, but *Romans* Writ:
So shall less Works, such as to-Night's slight Play,
At your Command, with Justice die away;
'Till then forgive your Writers, that can't bear⎫
You should such very *Tramontanes* appear,　⎬
The Nations, which contemn you, to revere. ⎭

Let *Anna's* Soil be known for all its Charms;
As Fam'd for Lib'ral Sciences, as Arms:
Let those Derision meet, who would Advance
Manners, or Speech, from *Italy* or *France*;
Let them learn You, you wou'd your Favour find,
And English be the *Language of Mankind*.

## The Mistake

## PROLOGUE,

### *Written by Mr.* Steele.

### Spoken by Mr. *Booth*.

Our Author's Wit and Raillery to-Night　⎫
Perhaps might please, but that your Stage-Delight⎬
No more is in your Minds, but Ears and Sight; ⎭
With Audiences compos'd of Belles and Beaux,
The first Dramatick Rule is, Have good Cloathes.
To charm the gay Spectator's gentle Breast,⎫
In Lace and Feather Tragedy's express'd,　⎬
And Heroes die unpity'd, if ill dress'd. ⎭

The other Style you full as well advance;
If 'tis a Comedy, you ask,—Who dance?
For oh! what dire Convulsions have of late
Torn and distracted each Dramatick State,
On this great Question, Which House first should sell
The New *French* Steps, imported by *Ruel?*
*Desbarques* can't rise so high, we must agree,
They've half a Foot in Height more Wit than we.
But tho' the Genius of our learned Age      }
Thinks fit to Dance and Sing, quite off the Stage, }
True Action, Comick Mirth, and Tragick Rage; }
Yet, as your Taste now stands, our Author draws
Some Hopes of your Indulgence and Applause.
For that great End this Edifice he made,
Where humble Swain at Lady's Feet is laid;
Where the pleas'd Nymph her conquer'd Lover spies, }
Then to Glass Pillars turns her conscious Eyes, }
And points a-new each Charm, for which he dies. }

The Muse, before nor Terrible nor Great,
Enjoys by him this awful gilded Seat:
By him Theatrick Angels mount more high,
And Mimick Thunders shake a broader Sky.

Thus all must own, our Author has done more
For your Delight, than ever Bard before.
His Thoughts are still to raise your Pleasures fill'd;
To Write, Translate, to Blazon, or to Build.
Then take him in the Lump, nor nicely pry
Into small Faults, that 'scape a busie Eye;
But kindly, Sirs, consider, he to-Day
Finds you the House, the Actors, and the Play:
So, tho' we Stage-Mechanick Rules omit,
You must allow it in a Whole-Sale Wit.

## Prologue to the University of *Oxford*.
### By Capt. *S——l.*

As wand'ring Streams by secret Force return
To that capacious Ocean whence they're born,
So for their Doom their Toils our Poets bring
To the fam'd[1] *Oxford* where they learnt to sing:[2]
These[3] happy Seats would rudest Minds inspire,
And all that see must feel Poetick Fire;
Aspiring Columns here, here beauteous Fields,
Here all that Art, here all that Nature yields,
Groves, Theatres, high Domes, and humble Shades,
Bright Palaces, and intermingled Glades,
Make the admiring Traveller debate
Whether they're form'd for Solitude or State;
While empty Pomp th' Inhabitants despise,
With whom alone 'tis Greatness to be wise.
Oh happy! and your Happiness who see!
Where Innocence and Knowledge can agree!

Ye calm Spectators of a guilty Age,
Pity the Follies of the World and Stage,
Free from what either act, or represent,
Weigh both the Character and the Intent,
And know Men as they are our Authors drew,
But what they should be, we must learn from you.

[1] great *1706*
[2] Then let the Learn'd their Visit not refuse,
Since what from you they gain, from us they loose.
For when around the Sacred Place we range,
Our Admiration we for Knowledge change.
We less adore their more exalted Vein,
And must expect a *Blenheim* or *Campaign*. (*Omitted from the 1707 text*)
[3] Such *1706*

## *The Distrest Mother*

### PROLOGUE,

Written by Mr. *Steele*.

Spoken by Mr. *Wilks*.

SINCE Fancy of it self is loose and vain,
The Wise by Rules, that airy Power restrain:
They think those Writers mad, who at their Ease
Convey this House and Audience where they please;
Who Nature's stated Distances confound,
And make this Spot all Soils the Sun goes round:
'Tis nothing, when a fancy'd Scene's in view,
To skip from *Covent-Garden* to *Peru*.
    But *Shakespear's* self transgress'd; and shall each Elf,
Each Pigmy Genius, quote Great *Shakespear's* self!
What Critick dares prescribe what's just and fit,
Or mark out Limits for such boundless Wit!
*Shakespear* could travel thro' Earth, Sea and Air,
And paint[1] out all the Powers and Wonders there.
In barren Desarts He makes Nature smile,
And gives us Feasts in his *Enchanted Isle*.
    Our Author does his feeble Force confess,
Nor dares pretend such Merit to transgress;
Does not such shining Gifts of Genius share,
And therefore makes Propriety his Care.
Your Treat with study'd Decency he serves;
Not only Rules of Time and Place preserves,
But strives to keep his Characters intire,
With *French* Correctness and with *British* Fire.
    This Piece presented in a Foreign Tongue,
When France was Glorious and her Monarch Young,

---

[1] ? *Misprint for* point

A hundred times a crowded Audience drew;
A hundred times repeated, still 'twas new.
   *Pyrrhus* provok'd, to no wild Rants betray'd,⎫
Resents his generous Love so ill repay'd;   ⎬
Does like a Man resent, a Prince upbraid.   ⎭
His Sentiments confess a Royal Mind,
Nor is he known a King from Guards behind.
   Injur'd *Hermione* demands Relief;
But not from heavy Narratives of Grief:
In conscious Majesty her Pride is shewn;
Born to avenge her Wrongs, but not bemoan.
*Andromache*—If in our Author's Lines,
As in the great Original, she shines,
Nothing but from Barbarity she fears:
Attend with Silence; you'll applaud with Tears.

## Prologue design'd for *Lucius* King of *Britain*, Written by Mrs. *Manley*.[1]

NAT. LEE—for Buskins fam'd—would often say,
To Stage-Success He had a certain Way;
Something for all the People must be done,
And, in[2] some Circumstance, each Order won;
This *He* thought easy, as to make a Treat,
And for a Tragedy gave this Receipt:

   Take me, said He, a Princess Young and Fair,
Then take a Blooming Victor flush'd with War;
Let him not owe, to vain Report, Renown,
But in the Lady's[3] Sight cut Squadrons down;
Let Him whom they themselves saw win the Field,
Him to whose Sword they saw whole Armies yield,
Approach the Heroine with dread Surprize,
And own no Valour Proof against bright Eyes:

[1] PROLOGUE, By Sir Richard Steele. *1717*
[2] with *1717*          [3] Ladies *1717*

The Boxes are Your own—the Thing is hit;⎫
And Ladies, as they near each other sit,       ⎬
Cry Ah,⁴ How movingly that Scene is writ!⎭
    For all the Rest, with Ease, Delights you'll shape,
Write for the Heroes in the Pit—a Rape:
Give the First Gallery a *Ghost*—on th' Upper,
Bestow, tho at this⁵ distance, a good *Supper*.
Thus, all their Fancies, working their own Way,
They're Pleas'd, and think they owe it to the Play.

    But the Ambitious Author of these Scenes,
With no low Arts to court your Favour means.
With Her Success, and Disappointment move,
On the just Laws of Empire, and of Love!⁶

    —In wanton Ease—ye *Britons*, learn to know,
Nor slight, in present Welfare, distant Woe!
Rescu'd from foreign Bonds, the happy Age
Sees no Abuse of Power, but on the Stage:
The *Briton* here, beholds the Tyrant bleed,
The Just thro' all the Mazes of their Fate succeed;
Our opening Earth, and our descending Sky,⎫
Our Bowl, our Dagger, ready Wrath supply,   ⎬
And, at the Poet's Nod, Kings reign or die.⎭
On such dire Forms, long shall this happy Isle,
As only Stage-Events, in Safety Smile;
While her great King magnificently spares,
Conquers, and wins, and Deeds of Grace prepares!
On *Dungeon*-Guilt, *He* Gleams of Mercy throws
And his each Action Heav'n's Vicegerent shows.

---

⁴ Oh *1717*        ⁵ that *1717*
⁶ *What follows Steele added in* 1720

# PROLOGUE:

Written by the Governor of the Comedians: Intended to be spoken when they acted at *Hampton-Court*, and began with a Comedy.

Howe'er we're wont to feign, we now appear
With true Concern, with undissembled Fear,
Our Disadvantage too, too well we know,
And here dare only Comic Humour show;
Our Tragic Pomps are for the World below.
They know not Sentiment from empty Rage,
When the Theatrick Monarch shakes the Stage;
Strides o'er his Realms with Scepter in his Hand,
By Heel and Feather, raising his high Stand,
Mantle and Train half covering his Command.
But Audiences, who weigh the Source of Things,
The Rise of Nations, and the Fate of Kings,
Detest an unexperienc'd, wild Essay,
And close examine, by the Life, a Play.
By such Stage-Heroes, with Contempt are seen,
Who swell with Rage, to form a Princely Mein.
The Counterfeit abhors a nearer View,
And Mimic Greatness dreads t'approach the True.
With easy, kind, familiar Power that reigns,
As Life informs our Frame, as Blood our Veins:
Terror and Noise spring from erroneous Force;
Thunder is an Offence in Nature's Course;
That bursts around, an empty Meteor forms,
It mounts in Vapours, and descends in Storms.
Nature's true Force is in calm Order seen;
Small Power is rough, Consummate is serene.
True Majesty's by smiling Virtue known,
Mix'd in a Crowd, attended, or alone
With conscious Goodness rais'd above its Throne.
Homage it loaths, delights to make Men free,
And raise the bended Suppliant from the Knee.

Rules not by stupid Pomp, but human Arts,
And, with the social virtues glads our hearts.
Smiles at our Follies, steals our Souls away,
And with our Wills, has arbitrary Sway.
Neglected Want, and friendless Merit trace, ⎫
In tender Features of a gracious Face; ⎬
Not the fierce Lord, but Friend of human Race: ⎭
As Grace and Favour Heav'n itself employs;
But, by its Angel's Ministring, destroys.
In gentle Acts of every passing Hour
The King diffuses, thro the Land his Power;
While conquering Arms and dreaded Fleets restrain
Rash distant Powers, and vindicate the *Main*.*

## *Prologue intended for* All for Love *Reviv'd*.

SINCE faint is Praise, which living Merit draws,
And always posthumous is true Applause;
Deny not Worth, far from your Eyes remov'd,
Its late Reward to be rever'd and lov'd.
To Poetry devoted be this Night,
And kill not, with your paltry Cares, Delight;
See how great *Dryden* could your Sires surprize,
E're Funds were giv'n, or Stocks could fall or rise,
E're Avarice had banish'd Love and Truth,
And with its vile Contagion seiz'd ev'n Youth;
When Vice had yet no other Fools to show,
But the well-natured Cully and the Beau:
'Twas *All for Love the World well lost* of old,
But now for Money better bought and sold.
    For Shame, that's only yours, which well you give;
Neglect not Life, only for means to live;
Look on yourselves, ye gaming Race, with Scorn,
And see what Images these Scenes adorn;

* Alluding to Admiral Bing. [*Steele's note*]

While Love and Fame alternately prevail,
As the great Master works the charming Tale.
Compare the generous Passions he excites,
To the fell Anguish of your gaming Nights,
When round pale Boards you sit with Feindlike pain,
For base Vicissitudes of Loss and Gain;
When Robbers, Beggars, Peers, with silent Hate,
And throbbing Breasts, to be each other, wait.
When thus our Bard (resist him if you can)
Has fairly from the Gamester won the Man;
Raise thyself still—and the past Times survey,
Since first the Age receiv'd this towring Play,
Since careless Luxury its Force could prove
In one Consent the World well lost for Love.
Reflect how Care pursues her thoughtless Hours,
And Fear the Adder lurking in the Flowers;
Think on great *WILLIAM*, *England's* Shame and Pride,
And how unthank'd, the toiling Hero dy'd,
On baffled Virtue, Fortune vainly kind,
Think on your Conquests to your Foes consign'd;
But think, though in tempestuous Seasons tost,
While Liberty is safe, the World not lost.


EPILOGUE [to the Town. Intended to be Spoken
in 1721.]

WHAT could our young Dramatic Monarch mean,
Now to revive this chaste old-fashioned Scene?
Did he project to make in this free Nation
A capital Offence of Fornication?
Thrice whimsical! who such wild[1] Plans espouses;
I'm sure, it ne'er wou'd pass thro' both the Houses.
'Tis what our Men scarce e'er think worth repenting,
And Women only Prudence not consenting.
But Eyes speak loud what's not pronounc'd by Lips,
Whil'st wide proclaiming Hoop scarce covers Hips.

[1] wise *1787*

This is the Tast our sad Experience shews;
This is the Tast of Belles as well as Beaux:
Else say, in *Britain* why shou'd it be heard,
That *Etherege* to *Shakespear* is preferr'd?
Whilst *Dorimant* to crowded Audience wenches,
Our *Angelo* repeats to empty Benches:
Our Nymph deluded has but coolly sped,
While to unwilling Bridegroom's Arms she's led;
*Loveit* unpitied mourns, unpitied wooes;
Still *Dorimant* triumphant Guilt pursues:
You've lost the Sense of giving Virgins Aid;
'Tis Comedy with you, an injur'd Maid:
The perjur'd *Dorimant* the Beaux admire;
Gay perjur'd *Dorimant* the Belles desire:
With fellow-feeling, and with[2] conscious Gust,
Each Sex applauds inexorable Lust.

For Shame, for Shame, ye Men of Sense, begin,
And scorn the base Captivity of Sin:
Sometimes at least to Understanding yield,
Nor always leave to Appetite the Field;
Love, Glory, Friendship, languishing must stand,
While Sense and Appetite have sole Command;
Give Man sometimes some Force in the Dispute;
Be sometimes Rational, tho oftner Brute.

Believe it, Sirs, if fit for us to say
Or if our Epilogue may suit our Play;
'Tis time, 'Tis time, ye should be more severe;
And what less guilty Nations suffer, fear;
Be Men, or hope not Heav'n will long secure ye
From quicker Pestilence than that round *Drury*.

[2] ? *Misprinted* well *1721*, *1787*

## *Tamerlane* Revived

### Prologue by Sir R. Steel.

### Spoken by a Lad in Girls Cloaths, before Tamerlane.

OLD Horace says, A Man who us'd t' expose
Coxcombs, bestow'd upon them gaudy cloaths.
Hence they'd grow wild & gay, Gallants profess,
And alter all their conduct with their Dress.
If such Ills 'rose from being but better clad,
What comes from dressing like a Girl, a Lad?
With my new Garb, I must confess the Change;
No more I think o'er Hedge & Ditch to range;
No: I grew nice, as I ungrew a boy,
And am a Lady—Delicate—& Coy.
Stand off Companions; I'm no more the same.
My Lips are Coral & my Eyes are flame.
No more I'll kick & Cuff who e'er advances,
But keep your distance, as you fear my Glances.
Behold with Awe, with Transport & Surprise
The Cupids in my Fan—& in my Eyes;
While I indifferent stand tho' deeply fir'd
With the Close bliss of being much admir'd.
Not all the Future Honours of the Gown
Should me my Fate reserve for such renown
Could on my rising thoughts such Joys bestow
As in my Female ornaments I know.
Tho I should wear in Learned Trappings vain
As Prelate, or as Chancellor my Train,
T'would be to scanty Dignity to stoop
After this Ample Petticoat & Hoop.

Epilogue by Sir R. Steel.

To Tamerlane, spoken by the Lad who acted Bajazet.

How hard t'will be to go to school again
After we have but for one night been Men!
Been Men! That's only growing taller things,
We have been Lovers, Generals, & Kings.
Again for word misplac'd or sentence skipt,
Shall Tamerlane or Bajazet be whipt?
Far be the thought—Freedom & Joy be Ours,
And ever banish't all Tyrannick Powers.
Freedom's which William's memory convey'd,
Great William is in Tamerlane display'd.
Faintly display'd! our Hero never knew
Conquest or Fortune to His Merit true.
In Tasteless Pomp an envy'd Crown he wore,
And a Long life in thankless labour bore.
Reward with praise, tho late, th' illustrious strife,
And give his name what you deny'd his life.
Still Rise his Fame as now it but began.
Be these scenes play'd thro every Race of Man.
That the glad Theme late ages may pursue,
We'll teach our Children what we learn from You.

# MISCELLANEA

# To Benjamin Hoadly, Bishop of Bangor.

VIRTUE with so much ease on Bangor sits
All faults he pardons, though he none commits.

# To Mrs. Manley.

AGAINST a Woman's Wit, 'tis full as low,
Your Malice, as your Bravery to Show.

# Rhymes in the Plays.

### *The Funeral*

AND Woman's happiness, for all her Scorn,
Is only by that Side whence she was Born.

### *The Lying Lover*

WE use all Arts the Fair to undermine,
And learn with Gallantry to hide Design.

FOR since through all the Race of Man we find,
Each to some darling Passion is Inclin'd,
Let Love be still the Bias of my Mind.

WHILE in a lovely Bowl I drown my Care,
She'll cease to be, or I to think her Fair.

### *The Tender Husband*

'TIS not the Lover's Merit wins the Field,
But to themselves alone the Beauteous yield.

THERE needs not time true passion to discover;
The most believing is the most a Lover.

THEY only who gain Minds, true Lawrels wear:
'Tis less to conquer, than convince, the Fair.


### *The Conscious Lovers*

THEY may be false who Languish and Complain,
But they who part with Money never feign.

To hope for perfect Happiness is vain,
And Love has ever its Allays of Pain.

TRUTH is too simple, of all Art bereav'd,
Since the World will—why, let it be deceiv'd.

WHATE'ER the generous Mind it self denies,
The secret Care of Providence supplies.


### *The School of Action*

WOULD you reform an heedless guilty age?
Adorn with virtuous characters the stage.


# Lines for a Poem by Another Hand.

WHEN all the Globe to Caesar's Fortune bow'd,
*Cato* alone his Empire disallow'd;
With Inborn Strength alone oppos'd Mankind,
With Heav'n in View, to all below it blind:
Regardless of his Friend's Applause or Moan,
Alone triumphant, since he falls alone.

# Lyric for Italian Music.

### I.

So notwithstanding heretofore
Strait forward by and by
Now everlastingly therefore
Too low and eke too high.

### II.

Then for almost and also why
Not thus when less so near
Oh! for hereafter quite so nigh
But greatly ever here.

# TENTATIVE
# ATTRIBUTIONS
# TO STEELE

## Anacreontique *to* Delia *on New-years-day.*

### *By Mr. S——*

AWAKE, awake, bright Nymph appear,
Give in a Glance my coming Year;
Faint Gleams of Light the Sphere adorn,
Open those Eyes, and help the Morn;
Begon, begon ye Shades away,
Her Curtain draws, and breaks the Day:
Behold the future Minutes strive
Which soonest shall at her arrive:
Some blissful, some afflicted be;
Be those for her, be these for me!
Yet let her so much Sorrow know,
As to conceive her Lovers Woe.
Dear Time into her Breast inspire
Tender Grief and soft Desire:
And if thou hear'st the humble Pray'r
Of Lovers dying in Despair,
On the Wise, and on the Grave,
On the Learned, on the Brave,
Who wou'd Names and Fortunes raise,
Good Time bestow thy Length of Days:
Let Length of Days their Portion be,
But give me Opportunity.

## *On his Mistress.*

### By a Parson.

WHEN the Three Charming Beauties of the Skies,
Contended Naked for the Golden Prize;
The Apple had not fall'n to *Venus* share,
Had I been *Paris*, and my *Delia* there.

In whom alone, we all their Graces find,⎫
The moving Gaiety of *Venus* joyn'd     ⎬
To *Juno's* Aspect, and *Minerva's* Mind.⎭
View but those Nymphs whom other Swains adore,
You'll value Charming *Delia* still the more.
*Dorinda's* Mien's Majestick; but her Mind
Is to Revenge, and Peevishness inclin'd.
*Myrtilla's* Fair, but yet *Myrtilla's* Proud.
*Cloe* has Wit, but Noisy, Vain and Loud.
*Melanea* doats upon the silliest Things,
And yet *Melanea* like an Angel sings.
But in my *Delia* all Perfections meet,
All that is Just, Agreeable and Sweet,
All that can Praise and Admiration move,
All that the Bravest and the Wisest love.

## Love's Relief.

A WRETCH long tortur'd with Disdain,
That hourly pin'd, but pin'd in vain;
At length the God of Wine addrest,
The Refuge of a wounded Breast.

Vouchsafe, oh Pow'r, thy healing Aid,
Teach me to gain the cruel Maid;
Thy Juices take the Lover's Part,
Flush his wan Looks, and chear his Heart.

Thus to the Jolly God he cry'd;
And thus the Jolly God reply'd,
Give whining o'er, be brisk and gay,
And quaff this sneaking Form away.

With dauntless Mein approach the Fair;
The Way to Conquer is to Dare.
The Swain pursu'd the God's Advice;
The Nymph was now no longer Nice.

She smil'd, and spoke the Sex's Mind;
When You grow Daring, We grow Kind;
Men to themselves are most severe,
And make us Tyrants by their Fear.


## To *Belinda*.

IN Church the Prayer-Book, and the Fan display'd,
And solemn Curt'sies, shew the wily Maid;
At Plays the leering Looks and wanton Airs,
And Nods and Smiles, are fondly meant for Snares.
Alas! vain Charmer, you no Lovers get;
There you seem Hypocrite, and here Coquet.


## *To* Flavia.

NATURE, in Pity, has deny'd you Shape,
Else how should Mortals *Flavia's* Chain escape?
Your radiant Aspect, and your rosie Bloom,
Without this Form would bring a Gen'ral Doom;
At once our Ruin and Relief we see,
At sight are Captives, and at sight are Free.


## On Nicolini's *leaving the Stage*.

BEGON, our Nation's Pleasure and Reproach!
*Britain* no more with idle Trills debauch;
Back to thy own unmanly *Venice* sail,
Where Luxury and loose Desires prevail;
There thy Emasculating Voice employ,
And raise the Triumphs of the wanton Boy.
Long, ah! too long the soft Enchantment reign'd,
Seduc'd the Wise, and ev'n the Brave enchain'd;

Hence with thy Curst deluding Song! away!
Shall *British* Freedom thus become thy Prey?
Freedom, which we so dearly us'd to Prize,
We scorn'd to yield it—But to *British* Eyes.

Assist, ye Gales; with expeditious Care
Waft this prepost'rous Idol of the Fair;
Consent, ye Fair, and let the Trifler go,
Nor bribe with Wishes adverse Winds to blow:
Nonsense grew pleasing by his *Syren* Arts,
And stole from *Shakespear's* self our easie Hearts.

## PROLOGUE,

### Design'd for Mr. D——'s last Play.

*Written by several Hands.*

GROWN Old in Rhyme, 'twere barbarous to discard
Your persevering, unexhausted Bard:
Damnation follows Death in other Men,
But your damn'd Poet lives and writes again.
Th' adventrous Lover is successful still,
Who strives to please the Fair against her Will:
Be kind, and make him in his Wishes easie,
Who in your own Despite has strove to please ye.
He scorn'd to borrow from the Wits of Yore;
But ever Writ as none e'er Writ before.
You modern Wits, should each Man bring his Claim,
Have desperate Debentures on your Fame;
And little would be left you, I'm afraid,
If all your Debts to *Greece* and *Rome* were paid.
From his deep Fund our Author largely draws;
Nor sinks his Credit lower than it was.
Tho' Plays for Honour in old Time he made,
'Tis now for better Reasons—to be Paid.

# POETICAL

# MISCELLANIES,

Confifting of

## *ORIGINAL POEMS*

### AND

## TRANSLATIONS.

*By the beſt Hands.*

---

Publiſh'd by Mr. *S T E E L E.*

---

## *L O N D O N*:

Printed for JACOB TONSON at *Shake-*
*ſpear's Head* over-againſt *Catherine-ſtreet*
in the *Strand*.   MDCCXIV.

Believe him, Sirs, h' has known the World too long,[1]
And seen the Death of much Immortal Song.
He says, poor Poets lost, while Players won,
As Pimps grow rich, while Gallants are undone.
Tho' *Tom* the Poet writ with Ease and Pleasure,
The Comick *Tom* abounds in other Treasure.
Fame is at best an unperforming Cheat;
But 'tis substantial Happiness to Eat——
Let Ease, his last Request, be of your giving,
Nor force him to be Damn'd to get his Living.

# The PROLOGUE at the *Opening of the Theatre-Royal, the Day After His* Majesty's *Publick Entry*. Spoken by Mr. Wilks.

AT length, *Britannia*, rescu'd from thy Fears,
Renew thy Joys: Thy promis'd King appears.
How did thy Sons, each Hour, with anxious Mind,
Consult the Skies, and importune the Wind!
How did they count each Wave, that caus'd his Stay,
Still rowling backward o'er the watry Way!
How did his Entry every Soul employ!
How strong the Transport! and how loud the Joy!

While You were zealous for your Soveraign's Right,
For Him we made our *Greeks* and *Romans* fight.
Oft as the Muse some God-like Hero drew,
Or set a virtuous Patriot to your View;
So oft we warm'd you in the *Brunswick* Cause,
And fix'd a generous People to their Laws.
Though great the Dearth of Comick Fools will be,
And a thin Crop of Coxcombs we foresee;
Though Sense is like to thrive throughout the Land,
And all *French* Fopperies will be Contraband:

---

[1] Believe him he has known the World too long, (Pope's *Miscellanies* 1727)

We not despair. Some Ridicule may rise,
Some modish Oddness, some bizarre Disguise:
So oft doth Rapture sober Sense destroy;
For Folly ever was the Child of Joy.
At least, for dear Variety, you'll chuse
Sometimes to listen to the Tragick Muse:
Here shall you sit, and solemn Silence keep,
Lest you grow Wanton, and forget to Weep.
When such a Monarch comes to bless the Age,
No Sorrows shall be felt, but from the Stage.

## PROLOGUE

*Spoken* at the Sensorium *on His* Majesty's *Birth-day*.

    For bright Assemblies, and for Tastes refin'd,
This Little Theatre was first design'd,
In which the well-pleased Founder hopes to treat
An Audience rather Elegant than Great;
While Wit and Beauty shall the Scene divide,
And charm each other, rang'd on either Side.
Fearful of noisy Claps and loud Huzza's
That drown the Poem which they mean to praise,
He begs you calmly to espouse his Cause,
Nor fright the Neighb'ring Barge-men with Applause.

    To please you here shall different Ages strive.
New Arts shall flourish, and the Old revive.
To the raw Tribe of Templars shall be shown,
The *Grecian* Gesture, and the *Roman* Tone;
*Virgil* shall be the Talk of every Beau,
And Ladies lisp the Charms of *Cicero*.
The Land shall grow Polite from You, who sit
In chosen Ranks, *the Cabinet of Wit*;
To You shall Bards their Virgin-Works reveal,
And hoarse contending Orators appeal;
For your Applause the Rival Arts shall sue
And Musick take its Melody from You.

With happy Omens we prepare the Way,
A noble Theme, and an Auspicious Day.
O Britain! grateful consecrate to Mirth
The Time that gave thy great DELIVERER Birth.
Long may this Day through many a circling Year
Distinguish'd in thy festivals appear;
And all thy Sons in its Return delight,
Like those who form this Loyal House to Night.

# NOTES

## The Procession (*p.* 3)

The Procession. A Poem on Her Majesties Funeral. By a Gentleman of the Army.—*Fungar inani Munere*—Virg. *London,* Printed for *John Whitlock* in *Amen-Corner* near *Stationers-Hall.* 1695. Small folio pamphlet with black-bordered title-page. Two pages of dedication and eight pages of text. Price 4*d.* Publication date, 5 April. Narcissus Luttrell's copy at Harvard is priced and dated on the title-page in his autograph; and the copy at the Huntington Library also has the notation on it, 'ye 5th Aprill 95'. The Dedication to Lord Cutts, unsigned, is dated March 19. 1694/5. A second issue of the elegy appeared in May 1695 (*Term Catalogues,* ed. Arber, ii. 550), which is in every way identical with the first except for the imprint on the title-page: 'Printed for *Thomas Bennet* at the *Half-Moon* in St. *Paul's* Church-yard. 1695.' Presumably on Whitlock's illness and death the sheets of this publication were taken over by Bennet, who issued the pamphlet without any alteration (copies at the University of Texas and the Huntington Library). With either title-page it is extremely rare, only a few copies being known to exist.

When *The Procession* was written Steele was a private soldier in the Duke of Ormonde's regiment, the Second Troop of Royal Horse or Life Guards, in which he had enlisted some time between 1692 and 1694. His dedication of the poem to John Lord Cutts was very plainly a bid for patronage, successful as it proved to be, for later in 1695 he entered the Coldstream or Second Regiment of Foot Guards, of which Cutts was colonel, and began living in Cutts's household as aide or private secretary. It was perhaps unusual to go from the Horse to the Foot Guards; but, if we read aright between the lines of the Dedication, we see that the idealistic young Steele was attracted to Cutts because of his versatility as soldier and man of letters: 'For a long time, Your most passionate admirer' it is signed. Cutts was famous for his reckless bravery in battle, and his volume of occasional poems had been dedicated to Mary, then Princess of Orange, in 1687. Steele's rank in the Coldstream Guards was for a time that of standard bearer, his first commission as ensign being dated 1697. But for several years before he was commissioned captain—in 1702 in the 34th Foot—he was called 'Captain'; and we may surmise that, like other gentlemen soldiers serving as guidons and standard bearers in the Life Guards, he had the brevet-rank of captain (see Clifford E. Walton, *History of the British Standing Army 1660–1700,* 1894, pp. 409, 443). The title continued to be used for many years after he left the army about 1707.

Steele's commemorative tribute to Queen Mary was written shortly after her funeral on 5 March, when the pageantry of the funeral procession was still a vivid memory. As a spectator, possibly having a part in the ceremonies with his regiment, he was deeply affected by the solemnity of

the occasion. His description of the procession, which moved from the
Palace of Whitehall to Westminster Abbey, corresponds closely to the
account given in the *London Gazette* (No. 3059, 4–7 March 1695). Near
the head marched three hundred poor women—'her first and deepest
Mourners'—followed by the Commons. Then came the House of Peers
with their Speaker, Lord Keeper Somers, praised by Steele here, as likewise many years later in the dedication to him of the first volume of the
collected *Spectator*, for his eloquence and probity. Next came 'the Mourning Horse' led by the striking and much-admired figure of Viscount
Villiers, who had been Master of the Horse to the deceased Queen; then
the open funeral chariot drawn by eight horses and bearing aloft the coffin
draped in purple velvet, with a Woman of the Bed Chamber at the head
and the foot—'the Ladies placed on High'. From among the titled mourning ladies who followed the funeral car, Steele would naturally single out
for mention the Countess of Derby, who was the granddaughter of the
first Duke of Ormonde, patron of his childhood, and sister of his present
colonel. The tolling of the bells, the sound of the guns at the Tower, fired
at minute intervals, and of the drums and trumpets deepened the gloom
and stirred the imagination of the young soldier. The Westminster choir
attended at the entrance of the Abbey, and with the burial in the Chapel
of King Henry VII, the procession was at an end. No part of the elegy was
more heartfelt than the tribute to William, prostrate and unable to be in
attendance, which concluded Steele's first appearance in print.

Before its second printing, this time under his name in his *Poetical
Miscellanies*, 1714 (published in December 1713), he gave the poem a
careful revision, omitting fourteen lines and making stylistic alterations in
eighteen or nineteen others. He may have had his own misgivings as to its
merit. There is no mistaking the contemptuous ridicule of a lampoon
probably written early in 1714: *Upon Mr. Steele's Incomparable Elegy on
the Death of Queen Mary. Publish'd Eighteen Years after it was Written*—
with the note, 'See Mr. Steele's *Miscellany*.' The author assumes that
'honest Dick' had kept his poem twice nine years:

> Thus long suppress'd, the Poem comes at last,
> Like tainted *Mutton* kept too long for Taste.
> Full of such fine Conceits as erst have hung
> Upon the Milk-maid's, or the Bell-man's Tongue.

The lampoon has a Swiftian ring; and though it is not included among
Swift's poetical works, it was doubtless conceived by a Tory enemy with a
similar viewpoint at about the time Swift published his satirical verses
'Address'd to Richard St—le, Esq.' (6 or 7 January 1714). It was printed
in 1720 as the introductory item in a hostile pamphlet entitled *The Crisis
of Honesty. Being An Answer to the Crisis of Property. In a Letter to
Sir R—— S——*; and in 1727 it was included in one of the Pope–Swift
*Miscellanea* volumes (ii. 39–40: Case, *Bibliography of English Poetical
Miscellanies, 1521–1750*, Item No. 343 (2)).

Other appraisals of *The Procession* are somewhat more favourable. Nathan Drake admired the passage 'which vividly represents the affliction of the poor for the loss they sustained by her death'. The best praise to be given the couplets, according to Dobson, is 'that they are loyal'. Aitken regarded it as a poem, which, 'though sometimes crude, came from the heart, and is full of patriotic feeling'. The reader of today will note the qualities associated with the mature Steele—his humane temperament, his bent towards social reform, and his Whiggism. One has only to read it at the same time with the many elegies of Mary to recognize a certain freshness and vividness of tone which sets it apart.

Reprinted:

*The Bee. A Collection of Choice Poems from Books and Manuscripts*, Part II. Printed by W. Hunter and sold by J. Noon, T. Sharpley, S. Popping, A. Boulter, 1715, pp. 25–27 (an excerpt entitled *Queen Mary*, forty-four lines; lower-case letters used at the beginning of the lines give it a modern appearance).

*Bayle's Dictionary*, London, 1738, iv. 396 (the first forty lines).

*A Select Collection of Poems*, ed. Nichols, 1780, iv. 1–12 (the entire text of 1714).

Nathan Drake, *Essays, Biographical, Critical, and Historical*, 1805, i. 44–45 (an excerpt of eighteen lines beginning 'The Poor, her first and deepest Mourners are').

G. A. Aitken, *Life of Steele*, 1889, i. 52 (the last twelve lines of the 1714 text).

The Dedication was reprinted by Edward Solly, *Notes and Queries*, 7 March 1885; by Aitken, *Life*, i. 50–51; and by Blanchard, *Correspondence*, 1941, pp. 440–1.

The text is that of 1714 collated with the first edition.

## To the Mirrour of British Knighthood (*p.* 11)

These couplets were printed in Commendatory Verses, On the Author of the Two Arthurs, and The Satyr against Wit; By some of his particular Friends [ed. by Thomas Brown?], 1700, folio, pp. 4–5. They were Steele's contribution to the collection of satirical squibs addressed to Sir Richard Blackmore upon the appearance of his poem, *Satyr against Wit*, a censorious judgement of the poets and would-be poets of the town; and they are our first evidence of his association with the wits at Will's Coffee House. Christopher Codrington, an Oxford schoolfellow, who seems to have been one of the leaders in the project, may have drawn Steele into it. But a strong motive for participation would be a desire to take up the cudgels for his friend Addison—and incidentally for the admired physician-poet, Dr. Samuel Garth, and James Smalwood, Chaplain to the First Regiment of Foot Guards. The couplet to which Steele replied reads:

> In G—— the Wit the Doctor has undone,
> In S——d the Divine, Heav'ns guard poor Ad—son (p. 8).

Blackmore, a physician of some standing, found time to write long heroic poems that did not impress the wits at Will's; Steele refers here to *Prince Arthur* (1695) and *King Arthur* (1697) in addition to the *Satyr*. In later years he—as did Addison—respected Blackmore for his sense of social responsibility and his Whig principles, and even praised his poetry.

In Blackmore's retaliation, *Discommendatory Verses*, 1700, folio, p. 6, the reply to Steele's couplets is labelled 'To the Noble Captain, who was in a Damn'd Confounded Pet, because the Author of the *Satyr against Wit* was pleased to pray for his Friend.' Steele's identity was probably known at once. Several copies of *Commendatory Verses* have 'Capt. Steel' written in the margin beside his lines (copy examined at the Folger Library); but his name was not printed with them until later, possibly not until 1711. The approximate time of their composition was late in 1699 or early in 1700, as is shown by the time-table of the pieces concerned: the *Satyr against Wit*, 1700 (published in November 1699); *Commendatory Verses*, 1700 (29 February, *Post Boy*); and *Discommendatory Verses*, 1700 (6 April, *Post Boy*).

Reprinted:

> *The Works of Mr. Thomas Brown* . . . 1707–11, iv, 1711, pp. 188–9, 'By Captain *Steel*.' Also in subsequent editions.
>
> Aitken, *Life of Steele*, 1889, i. 61–62.
>
> Richard C. Boys, *Sir Richard Blackmore and the Wits*, 1949, p. 76.

Text from *Commendatory Verses*, first edition.

## To Congreve on *The Way of the World* (*p.* 12)

Congreve's play was produced at Lincoln's Inn Fields during the first week or so of March 1700, the exact date not known, and printed by Tonson on the 25th (*London Gazette*, No. 3586). The poem was written between this date and 1701, presumably early in 1701, when it appeared in print. Certain touches in it may be interpreted to mean that the date of composition was in 1700 fairly near the time when the play was published. The first of the two anthologies in which it was printed was the miscellany of poems compiled by Charles Gildon entitled: A New Collection of Poems on Several Occasions. Written by Mr. *Dryden*. Mr. *Wolsly*. Mr. *Granville*. Mr. *Stepney*. Sr *Charles Sidley*. Sr *Fleet*. *Shepherd*. And several other Eminent Hands. Never before Publish'd. Printed for Peter Buck . . . and George Strahan. 1701. 8vo. pp. 335–9. The exact date of publication for this issue of Gildon's book has not been found, but it must have been early in 1701, for a second issue with a variant title-page—A New Miscellany of Original Poems—and with other variants, was advertised for 8–10 July

1701 (*Post Man*). The second anthology in which it was printed was Abel Boyer's collection of poetry and prose: Letters of *Wit, Politicks* and *Morality*. Written Originally in *Italian*, By the Famous Cardinal *Bentivoglio*; Also Select Letters of *Gallantry* . . . to which is added a large Collection of Original Letters of Love and Friendship. Written, By several Gentlemen and Ladies, particularly, . . . Mr. *Granville, Tho. Cheek*, Esq; Capt. *Ayloffe*; Dr. *G*——, Mr. *B*——*y*, Mr. *O*——*n*, Mr. *B*——*r*, Mr. *G*——, Mr. *F*——*r*, Mrs. *C*——*l*, Mrs. *W*——*n*. Printed for J. *Hartley* . . . W. *Turner* . . . Tho. *Hodgson*. 1701. 8vo. pp. 260–2. The Dedication is dated 5 July, and it was published 22–24 July (*Post Man*).

The poem was not printed in 1706 where one might expect to find it —in the second and revised edition of the *Way of the World*; but in Congreve's collected *Works* of December 1710 (three volumes, Tonson) it was used as the introductory item in vol. ii, which also contained, but not printed directly after the poem, the play in question. Finally it was included in Steele's *Poetical Miscellanies* of 1714, a book he dedicated to Congreve (pp. 162–4).

There are three textual versions: that of Gildon's volume; that of Boyer's volume; and the third and definitive version used in both Congreve's *Works* and Steele's miscellany. The Gildon form consists of 54 lines; the Boyer form has 50 lines; the third form has 50 lines—not identical, however, with those of the Boyer. The supposition is that for his collection Boyer doctored the Gildon version. The two couplets lacking in his version appear to be omissions from an original form rather than additions (see variant readings 7 and 20), and the seven or eight word variations in the Boyer form strongly suggest the hand of an 'improving' editor (see variants 3, 8, 9, 11, 12, 16, 17, 21). At any rate, when Steele cast the epistle in its final form, he retained the couplets omitted by Boyer and ignored the verbal alterations; he even followed the punctuation, capitals, and spelling of the Gildon. That is to say, a collation of the various forms indicates that the final revision of the epistle for Congreve's *Works* was based on the Gildon text. This, however, was subjected to quite a little change: the familiar *thee* and *thy* were dropped; having lost their timeliness and point, the four lines referring to 'Forgotten Authors' were omitted (variant 6); the metre in the troublesome first line was altered for the better; and several verbal alterations were made (variant readings 1, 10, 13, 15, 19).

In 1710 the two men were old acquaintances, and we may believe that the close scrutiny of his epistle upon Congreve's request was undertaken as a willing task. This third textual form was given the final stamp of approval and made definitive when it was printed verbatim, except for the correction of a misprint, in the *Poetical Miscellanies*.

Steele's epistle should be read, as it was written, against the background of Jeremy Collier's attack upon Congreve in *A Short View of the Immorality and Profaneness of the English Stage* and that of his anonymous detractors in the controversy that followed (1698–9). Congreve was sorely hurt by these attacks and annoyed without doubt by Blackmore's censorious tone in the *Satyr against Wit* (November 1699, dated 1700). It was at this time when Collier and his forces were berating him for the cynical pictures of society in his plays and when London audiences and critics were giving an icy reception to the *Way of the World* that Steele spoke out, the only one to do so in a public epistle, for Congreve and his play. Brushing aside with a casual reference 'Forgotten Authors who have lately Writ' and ignoring their charge of immorality, he takes the position that a more serious menace to the English stage is the craze of the audience, 'the Well-dress'd Barbarians', for spectacle and show. And by enlarging the scope of his commentary to include the whole of Congreve's work—'in ev'ry way of Writing to excell', he seems intentionally to have taken the spotlight away from the offending comedies.

Reprinted:

*A Select Collection of Poems*, ed. Nichols, 1780, iv. 14–17.

The text is that of *Poetical Miscellanies*, 1714, collated with the Gildon and Boyer versions, 1701, and the version of 1710.

## To Dr. Ellis (*p.* 14)

An epigram which Steele wrote on the fly-leaf of a copy of his first published essay—The Christian Hero: An *Argument* Proving That *No Principles but those of* Religion Are sufficient to make a Great Man. Second Edition, with Additions. Printed for *Jacob Tonson*. 1701. 8vo. (Published 17–19 July, *Post Boy*).

Dr. Welbore Ellis, afterwards Bishop of Kildare and of Meath, Steele's tutor at Oxford in the years 1689–91, was also Chaplain of the Second Troop of Horse Guards in which he began his army career. His gratitude to 'the Reverend Dr. Ellis, my ever Honour'd Tutor', is publicly expressed in the Preface of the book. The autographed presentation copy of the *Christian Hero* is at the Victoria and Albert Museum, Dyce Collection, South Kensington.

Reprinted:

*The Dyce and Forster Collections*, London, 1880, p. 22 (facsimile).

Austin Dobson, *Richard Steele*, 1886, p. 27.

Aitken, *Life*, 1889, i. 31.

*The Christian Hero*, ed. Blanchard, 1932 (facsimile).

Text from Steele's autograph.

## Horatian Ode, Applied to Marlborough (*p.* 14)

This first appeared in The Diverting Post. No. 2, 28 October to 4 November, 1704. Printed and sold by B. Bragg. Folio half-sheet. (Copy examined at the Folger Library: in Vol. I. For the Year 1705, London, 1706. Printed for Henry Playford and sold by John Nutt). The poem was written obviously shortly after the battle of Blenheim, and as we see Steele's printed eulogy of Marlborough preceded by a month Addison's *Campaign*, which appeared in December. His name was given with it in *Oxford and Cambridge Miscellany Poems*, 1708, in the Table as 'By Captain *Steel*'.

Reprinted:

> *Oxford and Cambridge Miscellany Poems*, ed. E. Fenton, Printed for Bernard Lintott, 1708, pp. 319–20. (Published 6–8 January, *Daily Courant*.)
>
> *Wit and Mirth or Pills to Purge Melancholy* [ed. Thomas D'Urfey?], 1714, v. 347. (Published 26 June, *Post Boy*.)
>
> *The Odes and Satyrs of Horace, That have been done into English by the most Eminent Hands*, Printed for Tonson, 1715, p. 15; 1717, p. 15.
>
> *Songs Compleat, Pleasant and Divertive*, ed. D'Urfey, Printed by W. Pearson for J. Tonson, 1719–20, iii. 351. (Published 26 March 1719, *Post Boy*.)
>
> *The Works of Horace in English Verse*, ed. William Duncombe, 1757, i. 26.
>
> *A Select Collection of Poems*, ed. John Nichols, 1780, iv. 13–14.
>
> *The Epistolary Correspondence of Steele*, ed. Nichols, 1809, ii. 616.

Text from the *Diverting Post*.

## Verses addressed to Addison (*p. 15*)

Addison's *Cato* was first acted at Drury Lane early in April 1713, possibly the 10th or the 14th, and was printed by Tonson on 27 April (*Guardian*, No. 40). Steele's verses headed a group of congratulatory poems, including those by Hughes, Young, Eusden, Tickell, Cotes, Philips, and an anonymous poet [George Jeffreys], first printed in the seventh edition, appearing on 26 June 1713 (*Guardian*, No. 92), 'This day the 7th edition . . . with copies of verses to the author prefixed': Cato. A Tragedy. As it is Acted at the Theatre-Royal in *Drury-Lane* by Her Majesty's Servants. By Mr. *Addison*. The Seventh Edition. For Jacob Tonson. 1713. 12mo. The prologue to the play was by Pope and the epilogue by Garth.

Reprinted:

> *The Works of Addison*, ed. Thomas Tickell, 1721, i. 261.
>
> *Epistolary Correspondence of Steele*, ed. John Nichols, 1787, ii. 389; 1809, i. 308.
>
> *Works of Addison*, ed. Bohn, 1862, i. 162.
>
> Aitken, *Life*, 1889, i. 372.

Text from *Cato*, 7th edition, collated with Tickell's edition.

### Songs in *The Funeral* (*pp.* 19–21)

Steele's play was produced in November or December 1701, the exact time not known, and printed on 20 December 1701 (*Post Boy*) with the date 1702 on the title-page: The Funeral: or, Grief A-la-mode. A Comedy. As it is Acted at the Theatre Royal in *Drury Lane*, By His Majesty's Servants. Written by Mr. *Steele*. Printed for Jacob Tonson. 1702. 4to.

An old Oxford acquaintance, Daniel Purcell, set four of the songs. Purcell, brother of the composer Henry, was organist at Magdalen College and was well liked by Steele possibly not so much for his music as for his jolly companionship (Bod. MS. Rawlinson D. 833, f. 169, as reported by Willard Thorp in *Songs from the Restoration Theatre*, 1934, p. 125). He had a hand in the music for all three of Steele's early plays. Two of the singers, when the play was first acted, were the virtuosos, 'Mr.' Pate and James Bowen; and a Mrs. Harris and the accomplished Mary Ann Campion sang in some of the early performances. The singing of 'Cynderaxa' was left to the tender mercies of William Pinkethman, who in the role of Soldier Trim romped through the merry verses with the kitchen tongs serving as lute. 'Honest Pinkey', the popular droll, also created the parts of the highwayman Storm in the *Lying Lover* and Humphry Gubbin, Biddy's country suitor, in the *Tender Husband*.

Special incidental music was composed for the play by William Croft and was printed separately shortly after the play was acted by John Walsh (16–18 December, *Post Boy*). The set of act-tunes is in eight sections—overture, Scotch aire, slow aire, jigg, slow aire, aire, aire, and chaconne—and is scored in four parts for first and second treble, tenor, and bass. The songs were frequently reprinted throughout the century in song-books and in miscellanies as lyrics to be read and recited. But they appeared anonymously and detached from their dramatic contexts, and as time passed words and even whole lines were altered, so that by the end of the century several had lost their original identity and Steele's name was no longer associated with them.

### 'Let not love on me bestow', II. iii.

*A Collection of the Choicest Songs and Dialogues Composed by the Most Eminent Masters of the Age*, folio, J. Walsh, [*c.* 1704], p. 112. 'Set by Daniel Purcell and Sung by Mrs. Harris.' Key of C major with figured bass [for harpsichord, spinet, or bass-viol]. A short concluding passage for the flute. (Folger Library.)

Thomas D'Urfey, *Wit and Mirth: or Pills to Purge Melancholy*, 1706, 1707, 1709, iv. 184–5; and in his *Songs Compleat, Pleasant, and Divertive*, 12mo, 1719–20, vi. 22–23. Purcell's setting, melody only. (Library of Congress.)

John Stafford Smith, *A Collection of Songs of Various Kinds and for*

*Different Voices*, [177–], p. 6. 'A Chearful Glee', set for three voices, two trebles and a bass. (Library of Congress.)

G. A. Aitken, *Life of Richard Steele*, 1889, ii. 372–4. Purcell's setting.

The words without music are found in *The Hive*, 1724, i. 201, as 'The Painful Part of Love Renounc'd'; *The Choice*, 1733, ii. 179; *The Lark*, 1740, p. 59; *The Thrush*, 1749, p. 213; *The Aviary*, [1744], p. 312; *The Warbling Muses*, 1749, p. 280; *The Charmer*, 1751, ii. 194; *The Vocal Magazine or Compleat British Songster*, 1784, No. 123; Joseph Ritson, *A Select Collection of English Songs with their Original Airs*, 1783, 1813, i. 136: with the note that 'it was set in a most labored, mechanical manner by Daniel Purcell, but his music was not thought worthy of insertion'; John Aikin, *Essays on Song-Writing with a Collection of Such English Songs as are Most Eminent for Poetical Merit*, [1772], 1810, p. 199, classified as 'a witty song'; Aikin, *Vocal Poetry*, 1810, p. 209.

### 'Ye minutes bring the happy hour', iv. ii.

*A Collection of the Choicest Songs and Dialogues*, [*c.* 1704], p. 213 (listed but missing from the Folger copy); [*c.* 1710], p. 192. 'Set by Daniel Purcell and Sung by Mrs. Campion.' With figured bass.

Aitken, op. cit. ii. 374–5.

The words without music are found in *The Choice*, 1733, ii. 179; *Vocal Miscellany*, 1734, i. 306; *The Syren*, 1735, p. 252; *The Cupid*, 1736, p. 55; *The Aviary*, [1744], p. 645; *The Charmer*, 1751, ii. 194. In several of these miscellanies Chloe's name becomes Phillis, and Corinna becomes Ardelia.

### 'Cynderaxa, kind and good', iv. ii.

I have found no trace of the music, but Mr. Harding has a note written some years ago, the authority now forgotten, to the effect that the composer was William Croft.

The words are given in *The Hive*, 1724, ii. 118; *The Choice*, 1733, ii. 180; *The Linnet*, 1749, p. 284; *The Warbling Muses*, 1749, p. 280; *The Charmer*, 1751, ii. 195; *Songs and Lyrics from the English Playbook*, [1945], p. 196, as 'The Fair Kitchen-maid'; *A Collection of Select Epigrams. Published by Mr. Hackett*, 1757, p. 30.

### 'On yonder bed supinely laid', v. iv.

*A Collection of the Choicest Songs and Dialogues*, [*c.* 1704], p. 130. (Folger Library); [*c.* 1710], p. 124. 'Set by Daniel Purcell.' With figured bass.

The words alone are given in *The Hive*, 1725, iii. 70; *The Choice*, 1733, ii. 180; *The Thrush*, 1749, p. 398; *The Warbling Muses*, 1749, p. 281.

'Arise, arise, great dead, for arms renowned', v. iv.

In the printed play Steele labelled the song, 'Set by Daniel Purcell'; but the music has not been found.

The words are given in *The Hive*, 1725, iii. 33; *A Complete Collection of Old and New Songs*, 1736, iv. 58; *Vocal Miscellany*, 1734, i. 310; *The Syren*, 1735, p. 234; *The Aviary*, [1744], p. 47; *The London Songster or Polite Musical Companion*, 1773, pp. 394–5; *The Vocal Magazine*, 1784, No. 1083; *The Masque*, [*c.* 178–], p. 80; F. S. Boas, *Songs and Lyrics from the English Playbook*, [1945], p. 196.

## Songs in *The Lying Lover* (*pp.* 21–23)

First printed in Steele's play The Lying Lover: or, The Ladies Friendship. A Comedy, As it is Acted at the Theatre Royal By Her Majesty's Servants. Written by Mr. *Steele.* Printed for Bernard Lintott, 1704. 4to. It was produced on 2 December 1703 and printed on 26 January 1704 (*Daily Courant*). Steele took his plot from *Le Menteur* (1642) by Corneille.

The composers of three of the songs are known: William Croft, Daniel Purcell, and Richard Leveridge. One of the notable musical features of the play was the contribution made by Leveridge, singer and composer, at this time a singing member of the Drury Lane Company. According to the printed text he sang in the first run 'Venus has left her Grecian Isles' and 'The rolling years'; and the song-sheet version provides evidence that he both set and on occasion sang 'Since the day of poor man' in the theatre or the concert-hall. This particular song was intended for Bookwit; and undoubtedly Robert Wilks, who created the part, must also have sung it. He had a good voice and, as Ensign Campley and Captain Clerimont, would also be called upon for certain songs in the *Funeral* and the *Tender Husband*. William Croft composed a set of act-tunes for the *Lying Lover*, which like his music for the *Funeral* was used for special effects within the play itself. It is scored as is the *Funeral* music in eight sections: overture, hornpipe, aire, round O slow, aire, trumpet aire, minuet round O, and chaconne. The first casts included players who could dance and sing, as well as the comedians Pinkethman, Norris, and Bullock; and Croft's music undoubtedly added lively effects to Steele's comedies. The set for this play was published by John Walsh on 21–23 December 1703 (*Post Man*).

'Thou soft machine that dost her hand obey', ii. i.

*The Monthly Masks of Vocal Musick*, 2 pp., April 1704. 'A Song to Celia's Spinnett. Sett by M$^r$ William Crofts.' With figured bass. Symphony at the end 'For the flute'. (Houghton Library.)

The words are given in *The Hive*, 1725, iii. 12.

'Venus has left her Grecian isles', III. ii.

'A Song by M^r Leveridge. Sett by M^r Dan: Purcell', folio, double sheet, 2 pp., [n.d]. Key of A major with figured bass [for harpsichord, spinet, or bass-viol]. Symphony at the end 'For the flute'. (Library of Congress.)

*The Monthly Masks of Vocal Musick, Containing all the Choicest Songs by the Best Masters Made for the Playhouses, Public Consorts, and Other Occasions*, folio, J. Walsh, July, 1704. The score is that described above. (Houghton Library, Harvard University.)

The words without music are given in *The Choice*, 1733, iii. 25; *The Warbling Muses*, 1749, p. 283, the first line changed to 'blissful isles' and the heroine to Florella.

### 'Since the day of poor man', IV. iii.

*The Monthly Masks of Vocal Musick*, July 1707. 'A Song Set and Sung by Mr. Leveridge.' In the key of E minor, with figured bass. With an instrumental passage between stanzas for the bass and a concluding symphony 'For the flute'. (Houghton Library and Library of Congress.)

*A Collection of Songs by Mr. Richard Leveridge*, folio, J. Walsh, [c. 1723], p. 32. (In Mr. Harding's Collection.)

*A Collection of Songs with the Musick by Mr. Leveridge, Engraved and Printed for the Author. With a Frontispiece Designed and Engraved by Hogarth*, octavo, 1727, two vols. in one, ii. 3. 'Life a Bubble.' Treble and bass. The score differs slightly from the *Monthly Mask* music. (Boston Public Library.)

*The Merry Musician or a Cure for the Spleen*, J. Walsh, [c. 1729], p. 159. 'Life a Bubble by Mr. Leveridge.' Melody only. (Boston Public Library.)

Aitken, op. cit. ii. 377–8. The score as given in the edition of 1727.

The words are given in *The Hive*, 1732, iv. 39 as 'Life Improved' and in *The Warbling Muses*, 1749, p. 283. With five additional six-line stanzas the poem is found in *Collection of Bacchanalian Songs*, 1729, p. 14; *The Choice*, 1733, iii. 13; *The Syren*, 1735, p. 268; *The Aviary*, [1744], p. 439; *The Robin*, 1749, p. 46.

### 'The rolling years the joys restore', v. iii.

In the printed play Steele labelled it 'Song by Mr. Leveridge', but no information concerning the setting or the composer has been found.

The words are given in *The Choice*, 1733, iii. 26; *The Syren*, 1735, p. 272; *The Aviary*, [1744], p. 491; *The Robin*, 1749, p. 119.

## Songs in *The Tender Husband* (*pp.* 23–26)

Steele's play was produced on 23 April 1705 and printed on 9 May (*Daily Courant*): The Tender Husband; or, The Accomplish'd Fools. A Comedy. As it is Acted at the Theatre-Royal in *Drury-Lane*. By Her Majesty's Servants. Written by Mr. *Steele*. Printed for Jacob Tonson, 1705. 4to.

These songs were fortunate in having an accomplished group of composers and singers for the first run of the play and another group for its
revival in the middle years of the century. Daniel Purcell composed settings
for both 'Gentle Parthenissa' and 'Why, lovely Charmer', the latter sung
by Mr. Francis (?) Hughes, counter-tenor, play-house musician, and opera
singer. A French musician, Lewis Ramondon, composer and opera singer,
set 'With studied airs' and sang it in 1706 as Mrs. Clerimont's spinet-
master. The music for all three songs required trained voices.

Later on in the 40's and 50's new and interesting settings were composed
for 'Lovely Charmer' by an anonymous composer and for 'Gentle Parthenissa' by Dr. Thomas Arne and a 'Mr.' Sullivan, a play-house musician.
Dr. Arne's setting was sung by Mrs. Clive, who at several performances
acted the part of Biddy Tipkin. The perennial revivals of the play helped
to keep the songs alive, as did the demand for new songs for the musical
entertainments at the pleasure gardens of Vauxhall, Marylebone, and
Ranelagh. John Barrett composed the act-tunes for the play, which were
printed and sold at '1s. 6d. the set' by John Walsh about the 8th of May
1705 (*Post Man*).

### 'See, Britons, see with awful eyes'

This song follows the Prologue in the printed play and has the heading,
'A Song Designed for the Fourth Act, but not Set.' The only song-book
reference found is in *The Choice*, 1733, iii. 23.

### 'With studied airs and practised smiles', iii. i.

*The Monthly Masks of Vocal Musick*, 2 pp., May 1706. 'A Song in the
Tender Husband. Sett and Sung by Mr Ramondon at the Theatre Royal.'
With instrumental passages at the beginning and between stanzas for the
bass; symphony at the end 'For the flute'. (Houghton Library.)

A song-sheet edition of the item described above, folio, double sheet,
2 pp., [n.d.]. (Houghton Library: Mus. 505.7 F*, sheet music.)

The words are given in *The Hive*, 1724, i. 24 under the title 'The Artful
Mistress'; *The Choice*, 1733, iii. 21; *The Warbling Muses*, 1749, p. 281,
where the heroine becomes Celia.

### 'Why lovely charmer, tell me why', iv. i.

*The Monthly Masks of Vocal Musick*, May 1705. 'A Song in the Tender
Husband, Sung by Mr Hughes. Set by Mr. Dan: Purcell. Within the
Compass of the Flute.' Opening line: 'Why, Belvidera, tell me why'. With
figured bass [for the harpsichord, spinet, or bass-viol]. (Houghton Library.)

*The Musical Miscellany. A Collection of Choice Songs Set to the Violin
and Flute*, small octavo, J. Watts, 1729–31, i. 170. Words only with the
statement that the song can be sung to Mr. Green's [Maurice Greene]

setting of 'Did ever swain a nymph adore' or *Robin's Complaint*, the melody
given on p. 168. (Boston Public Library.)

*The Vocal Miscellany*, 1734, p. 316. Words only with the statement that
the song can be sung to the tune of 'Gently touch the warbling lyre'. These
words are by Arthur Bradley and the music is Geminiani's *Minuet*, given
in *Musical Miscellany*, i. 49.

*A Collection of English Songs*, folio, [175–], i. 55. 'A New Song.' This
is a different setting from that in the *Monthly Masks*. Composer's name not
given. With figured bass and a symphony 'For the flute'. (Boston Public
Library.)

'A New Song', folio, single sheet, [n.d.]. Like the preceding item. (Julian
Marshall Collection of Sheet Music: Houghton Library.)

The words without the music are found in *The Hive*, 1724, i. 249 as
'The Nonplus' and in ii. 131 as 'To His Various Mistress'; *The Syren*,
1735, p. 271; *The Cupid*, 1739, p. 60; *The Choice*, 1733, iii. 22; *The
Musical Companion*, 1741, p. 218; *The Aviary*, [1744], p. 622; *The
Warbling Muses*, 1749, p. 282, where 'lovely charmer' becomes 'Sweet
Inchantress'; Aikin, *Vocal Poetry*, 1810, p. 176; *The Book of English Songs*,
1851, p. 56; E. B. Reed, *Songs from British Drama*, 1925, p. 225; F. S.
Boas, *Songs and Lyrics from the English Playbook*, [1945], p. 197, as 'So
very kind, and yet so shy?'

## 'While gentle Parthenissa walks', IV. ii.

*The Monthly Masks of Vocal Musick*, April 1705. 'A Song by the Boy in
the Tender Husband. Set by Mr Daniel Purcell. Within the compass of
the Flute.' Treble and bass. Key of B flat major. (Houghton Library.)

*The Musical Miscellany*, 1731, vi. 163. Words only with the statement
that they can be sung to 'Fame of Dorinda's conquests brought', a song by
John Hughes, music by Dr. Pepusch, given on p. 161.

*London Magazine*, 1745, p. 302. 'A Song Set by Mr. Sullivan.' The
first line reads: 'When gentle Parthenissa . . .'.

*Universal Harmony*, octavo size, J. Newbery, 1745, p. 92. Ornamental
head-piece. 'Sung by Mr. Sullivan.' With figured bass; introductory and
concluding instrumental passages. (Library of Congress.)

*Amaryllis*, octavo size, 1746, p. 60. 'Sung and Set by Mr. Sullivan.'
(Boston Public Library.)

*A Collection of English Songs*, folio, [175–], i. 117. 'Gentle Parthenissa.
Set by Mr. Sullivan.' With figured bass. Symphony at the end 'For the
German flute'. (Boston Public Library.)

*Apollo's Cabinet or the Muses Delight*, octavo size, Liverpool, 1756, i.
112. 'Sung by Mr. Sullivan.' (Boston Public Library.)

Thomas Augustine Arne, *The Songs in the Comedies Called As You Like
It and Twelfth Night . . . with Another in the Tender Husband*, folio,
W. Smith, [1745–50], p. 2. 'When gentle . . . Sung by Mrs. Clive.' Scored

in three clefs: violin (?), voice, and figured bass. Transposed for the German flute, p. 21. (Folger Library.)

*The Delightful Pocket Companion for the German Flute*, J. Simpson, [1745], ii, No. 20. Arne's music without the words. (Library of Congress.)

*Songs. Francis Hopkinson His Book*, oblong folio, manuscript, Philadelphia, 1759, p. 124. Arne's music with harpsichord accompaniment. (Library of Congress.)

Benjamin Martin, *Miscellaneous Correspondence*, octavo, 1759, ii. 739 (for Feb. 1758). 'Whilst in the Grove Timandra Walks. A New Song by Mr. Bagley.' Treble and bass. (Houghton Library.)

Aitken, op. cit. ii. 378–81, Purcell setting; ii. 382–4, Arne setting.

The words without music in *The Hive*, 1724, ii. 113, as 'The Irresistable Charmer'; *The Choice*, 1733, iii. 22; *The Syren*, 1735, p. 271; *The Robin*, 1749, p. 293; *The Aviary*, [1744], p. 608; *The Warbling Muses*, 1749, p. 282, where the first line becomes 'Whilst in the grove Timandra walks'.

## A Song in *The Conscious Lovers* (p. 26)

Steele's comedy was first produced on 7 November 1722 and was printed on 1 December (*Daily Courant*) with the date 1723 on the title-page: The Conscious Lovers. A Comedy. As it is Acted in Drury Lane, By His Majesty's Servants. Written by Sir Richard Steele. Printed for J. Tonson, 1723. 4to.

Two years before the production of the play Steele printed the song in his periodical *The Theatre* No. 18, 1 March 1720. This text differs slightly from that given in the Preface of the play, where it is accompanied by the statement that it was intended to be used in Act II as entertainment for Indiana but had to be omitted in the first run 'for want of a performer'. The song had four musical settings: the first was composed by John Ernest Galliard about 1720 when the play was being written; what seems to be the second was made by Dr. Samuel Howard for a revival of the play at Covent Garden in 1737; the third by an unknown musician, to judge from the score and the appearance of the song-sheet, was composed in the middle years of the century. All three settings were issued anonymously. The fourth, extant in manuscript form, was composed by the brilliant Italian musician Venanzio Rauzzini, operatic singer and composer, who came to England late in the century. Daniel Purcell had died in 1717 else he doubtless would have been called upon to help with this last play as he had with the others. It seemed to give Steele pleasure, however, to have the assistance of Galliard, with whom he had once been associated in the household of Prince George of Denmark. He would also have liked the simple tune by Howard, who, Dr. Burney said, 'preferred the style of his own country to that of any other'. But having all his life deplored the vogue and influence of foreign music, Steele might have been chagrined at the honour bestowed upon his song by Rauzzini.

The original intention for its performance must have been realized many times, as play-bills for the comedy, often revived, usually announced singing in the Second Act. Popular favourites such as Thomas Lowe, John Beard, Master Mattocks, and Miss Isabella Young were the singers. The words were adapted and sometimes sung to an air composed by George Monro for 'My goddess Celia heav'nly fair'. It may be added here that other of these play-songs were sung to melodies by Maurice Greene, J. C. Pepusch, and Francesco Geminiani.

That Steele himself thought well of *Indiana's Song* we see from his comment in the *Theatre* paper and the Preface. It probably mattered little to him that John Dennis was scornful of it in his hostile criticism of the play: 'I cannot help saying a Word to his Song . . . which he has brought in . . . for no other End, than to shew that he is as notable at Meter as he is at Prose' (*Remarks on the Conscious Lovers*, 1723, in *Works of Dennis*, 1943, ii. 260). The final verdict of the century, however, expressed by Nathan Drake, seems to have been favourable:

> . . . amatory lines, which, as they are written with much sweetness and delicacy both of sentiment and versification, are worthy of transcription (*Essays, Biographical, Critical, and Historical*, 1805, i. 143).

Text from the play collated with the *Theatre*, folio issue.

### 'From place to place forlorn I go', designed for ii. ii.

*The Musical Miscellany*, 1729, i. 104–5. 'Sung in the Conscious Lovers.' Composer's name not given; but as it is in company with ten other songs set by Galliard and is written in a similar style, this is conjectured to be the Galliard setting. Melody only, with short concluding passage 'For the flute'.

*Calliope or English Harmony*, octavo, J. Simpson, [*c.* 1737–9], i. 10. 'A Song in the Conscious Lovers.' Composer's name not given. Treble and bass, in Key of G minor. Concluding passage for the flute. Headed by engraved vignette. This is a different setting from that in *Musical Miscellany*. (Boston Public Library.) Composed by Samuel Howard? In a performance of the play at Covent Garden on 17 March 1737 the song was 'new set to Musick by Mr. Howard and sung by Mr. Beard' (*London Daily Post and General Advertiser*). *Calliope* contains other music by Howard.

'Indiana's Song in the Conscious Lovers', Engraved by Thomas Cross, s. sh. folio, [n.d.] (Chetham Library.) Same score as in *Calliope* and presumably that listed in the *Catalogue of Printed Music in the British Museum*.

'A Song with Symphony for the Entertainment of Indiana in the Conscious Lovers', folio, double sheet, 2 pp., [n.d]. Composer's name not given. Treble and bass. With instrumental introduction, interlude passages, and symphony at the end 'For the flute'. This is a third setting. (Julian Marshall Collection of Sheet Music: Houghton Library.)

Joseph Ritson, *A Select Collection of English Songs*, 2nd ed. 1813, words in i. 179; melody in iii. 91. Same air as in *Musical Miscellany*.

Aitken, op. cit. ii. 384–5. 'Indiana's Song, Composer not known.' Same score as in *Calliope*.

Venanzio Rauzzini, 'From place to place forlorn. From the *Conscious Lovers*. With strings.' Add. MSS. 31817, f. 84. From a collection made by R. J. S. Stevens about 1797. Listed in the *Catalogue of Manuscript Music in the British Museum*, ii. 365. This is the fourth setting. (Not seen by the present editor.)

Ursula Greville, *Charming Sounds: a Volume of Early Eighteenth-Century Songs. Arranged with Pianoforte Accompaniment by Owen Mase*, folio size, 1926, p. 9. 'Words and melody anonymous.' Same air as that in *Musical Miscellany*. (Boston Public Library.)

The words are given in *The Theatre*, No. 18, 1 March 1720, by Steele. *The Hive*, 1724, i. 112, as 'The Bashful Virgin'; *The Cupid*, 1736, p. 21 and 1739, p. 18, where it is stated that the song can be sung to 'My goddess Celia heav'nly fair', setting by Mr. Monro (to be seen in *Musical Miscellany*, 1730, iv. 124–5); *The Choice*, 1733, ii. 178; *The Nightingale*, 1738, p. 293; *The Musical Companion*, 1741, p. 213; *The Aviary*, [1744], p. 175; *The Linnet*, 1749, p. 378; *The Buck's Bottle Companion*, 1775, p. 13; *The Vocal Magazine*, 1784, No. 1148; Aikin, *Essays on Song-Writing*, 1810, p. 143, and *Vocal Poetry*, 1810, p. 134.

## Verses on Mrs. Selwyn (*p.* 32)

This poem is preserved in the Blenheim MSS. in Steele's autograph, written on a scrap of paper bearing the date 1694. The lady to whom the gallantry is addressed may have been a member of the notable military family, possibly the wife or daughter, of Colonel William Selwyn (1650–1702; of Matson, Gloucestershire). Selwyn, Colonel of the Second or Queen's Regiment of Foot, served with distinction in the campaign of 1693 and following the siege of Namur in 1695 was promoted to Brigadier-General. Later he was appointed Governor of Jamaica (Dalton, *English Army Lists and Commission Registers 1661–1714*, 1896, i. 287 and iii. 192). In 1694 Steele, aged 22 and a private in the Duke of Ormonde's Second Regiment of Royal Horse Guards, possibly had social contacts with the Selwyn family. If so the valentine may have been addressed to the wife, Albinia, or less likely to the daughter, Albinia, who then would have been only a child of twelve or thirteen years.

Printed:

Aitken, *Life*, 1889, i. 48.

Text from the manuscript.

## Two Poems in *The Muses Mercury* (*pp.* 32–33)

*To a Young Lady who had Marry'd an Old Man*
*Song*

The Muses Mercury: or, Monthly Miscellany. Consisting of Poems, Prologues, Songs, Sonnets, Translations, and Other Curious Pieces, Never before Printed. By the Earl of *Roscommon*, Mr. *Dryden*, Dr. *G——th*, *N. Tate*, Esquire, Mr. *Dennis*, Dr. *N——n*, Capt. *Steel*, Mr. *Manning*, &c. . . . Printed by *J. H.* for Andrew Bell. 1707. 4to. Dedication signed J.[ohn] O.[ldmixon]. The first poem appeared in the January issue, pp. 17–18 (published on 10 February). See the note to *Occasion'd upon Sight of Mrs. N.——n* for comment on the nature and purpose of the *Muses Mercury*, pp. 109–10.

The second poem appeared in the issue for February, p. 52 (published on 18 March).

Reprinted:

*Epistolary Correspondence of Steele*, ed. Nichols, 1809, i. 92 n.

*The Oxford Book of Eighteenth-Century Verse*, ed. D. N. Smith, 1926, No. 20.

*Poems on Several Occasions. Written in the Eighteenth Century*, ed. Kathleen W. Campbell, 1926, pp. 12–13.

Texts from *The Muses Mercury*.

## Epigrams adapted from Martial (*pp.* 33–35)

Martial provided mottoes for several of Steele's papers—*Spectator* Nos. 38, 49, 143, 158, 240; *Tatler* Nos. 94, 227, 260; *Guardian* No. 1. Translations of four epigrams are given in the *Tatler* and *Spectator*:

(1) *Lib.* 1. *Ep.* 13. *Tatler* No. 72, 24 September 1709.

To meet the request of a correspondent Steele relates the story of Paetus and his wife Arria and concludes with the remark: 'The Woman's Part in this Story is by much the more Heroick, and has occasion'd one of the best Epigrams transmitted to us from Antiquity.'

(2) *De Vetula*, an epigram attributed to Martial. *Spectator* No. 52, 30 April 1711.

Steele's comment: 'An Epigram a smart Fellow writ . . . his Malice is stolen from *Martial*.'

Reprinted:

*Collection of Epigrams* [ed. William Oldys?]. Printed for Walthoe, 2nd ed., 1735–7, i, No. 192: anonymous with the note, 'This is imitated from Martial very happily.'

*Select Epigrams of Martial Translated and Imitated by William Hay . . .
and Other Hands,* 1755, p. 231 (anonymous).

*Select Epigrams,* 1797, ii. 122 (anonymous).

(3) *Lib.* 1. *Ep.* 68. *Spectator* No. 113, 10 July 1711.

At the conclusion of a paper on Sir Roger's infatuation for the Widow,
Steele offers a translation of 'the Epigram which represents with much
Humour my honest Friend's Condition'.

Reprinted:

*Collection of Epigrams,* Printed for Walthoe, 1727, No. 299; 2nd ed.
1735–7, No. 297 (anonymous).

*Select Epigrams by William Hay,* 1755, p. 219 (anonymous).

*The Festoon. A Collection of Epigrams Ancient and Modern,* ed. Richard
Graves, 2nd ed. 1767, p. 62 (anonymous).

*Select Epigrams,* 1797, ii. 46 (with Steele's name).

*Poetical Farrago,* 1794, i. 168 (attributed to Addison).

*The Epigrams of Martial . . . Each Accompanied by Verse Translations,*
1875, p. 60 ('From the *Spectator*').

(4) *Lib.* 4. *Ep.* 22. *Spectator* No. 490, 22 September 1712.

Steele's introduction is 'I am pleased with an Epigram of *Martial* in
Honour of the Beauty of his Wife *Cleopatra*'.

Reprinted:

*A Select Collection of Poems with Notes,* ed. Nichols, 1780, iv. 18 (with
Steele's name).

Texts from the *Tatler* and *Spectator*, folio, collated with first collected
editions.

## Toasts for the Kit-Cat Club (*p.* 35)

These verses for the toasting glasses are preserved in the Blenheim MSS. in
a draft holograph letter from Steele to his secretary, Leonard Welsted,
dated 24 January 1716 and containing the direction: 'I have writ three
Couplets for the Toasts. They are to be printed under the names for the
Kitt Catt Club. These are the verses.' On the fly-leaf of the letter are five
toast couplets in another hand, with revisions in Steele's writing; but there
is no way of telling whether they were Steele's, dictated to an amanuensis,
or were someone else's submitted for his criticism. First line: 'Ye fair,
whose charms on chrystall records rise.'

Reprinted:

*Eighth Report of the Historical Manuscripts Commission,* 1881, *Appendix,*
Part 1, p. 24*a*.

Austin Dobson, *Richard Steele*, 1886, p. 53.
*Correspondence*, 1941, p. 110.

Text from the manuscript.

## Song (*p. 35*)

These verses were included in No. 9, 13 February 1716, of Steele's periodical: *Town-Talk, in a Letter to a Lady in the Country*. In the narrative framework of the paper—which was written by Steele—Arthur, the young lover, addresses his sweetheart Amorett in a letter and encloses the poem with the remark: 'I have given Imagination so much Liberty as to fancy I ruffl'd a Kiss from you, when a Country-Girl, and carried this to a Poetical Licence of writing the following Song on the Imaginary Occasion.'

Text from *Town-Talk*, original issue.

## Prologue and Epilogue to *The Funeral* (*pp. 39–41*)

For the facts of publication and production of Steele's play in 1701–2 see p. 80. Robert Wilks spoke the prologue in the role of Ensign Campley and Colley Cibber the epilogue as Captain, Lord Hardy.

Reprinted:
In subsequent editions of the play.
*Prologues and Epilogues Celebrated for their Poetical Merit*, Oxford, c. 1790.

Text from the first edition.

## Prologue and Epilogue to *The Lying Lover* (*pp. 41–42*)

For the facts of production and publication of Steele's play in 1703–4 see p. 82. The speakers are not designated.

Reprinted:
In subsequent editions of the play.
*Prologues and Epilogues Celebrated for their Poetical Merit*, Oxford, c. 1790.

Text from the first edition.

## Epilogue to *The Tender Husband* (*p. 42*)

For the facts of publication and production of Steele's third play in 1705 see p. 83. At the first performance Richard Estcourt spoke the epilogue in the role of Pounce. Of Estcourt Steele said at the time of his death: 'this extraordinary man, in his own way, never had an equal in any age before him or in that wherein he lived' (*Spectator* No. 468). The play was dedicated to Addison, who contributed a prologue that was spoken by Robert Wilks as Captain Clerimont.

Reprinted:

In subsequent editions of the play.

*Prologues and Epilogues Celebrated for their Poetical Merit*, Oxford, *c.* 1790.

*Original Prologues, Epilogues, and Other Pieces Never before Printed* . . . *to which is added a Collection of Such as are Celebrated for Wit, Humour, or Entertainment*, 1756, p. 23 (excerpt).

Text from the first edition.

## Prologue to *The Mistake* (*p.* 43)

First printed in John Vanbrugh's play: The Mistake. A Comedy. As it is Acted at the Queen's Theatre in the *Hay-Market*. By Her Majesty's Sworn Servants. By the Author of *The Provok'd Wife*, &c. London, Printed for Jacob Tonson, 1706. 4to.

It was produced on 27 December 1705 and printed on 11 January 1706 (*Daily Courant*). Barton Booth was the speaker of the prologue in the role of Don Carlos. The epilogue was written by Peter Motteux. Vanbrugh's own theatre in the Haymarket had been opened in April 1705, and the *Mistake* was acted there during the time of his management. 'Finds you the House, the Actors, and the Play' is Steele's line saluting Vanbrugh as architect, production manager, and playwright.

Reprinted:

*Prologues and Epilogues Celebrated for their Poetical Merit*, Oxford, *c.* 1790.

Text from the first edition.

## Prologue to the University of Oxford (*p.* 45)

Prologue to the University of *Oxford*. Written by Mr. *Steel*, and spoken by Mr. *Wilks*. Printed for Bernard Lintott. London, 1706. Price 2*d*. Folio half-sheet. Printed in June or July (*History of the Works of the Learned* for June and 'this day', *Daily Courant*, 4 July). A copy is preserved in the Chetham Library, Manchester, Halliwell-Phillipps broadside No. 94 (see frontispiece, reproduced with the kind permission of the Feoffees of the Library). In 1707 the broadside version of 1706 was reprinted in a revised form in the *Muses Mercury*. Steele made two verbal changes and judiciously omitted a passage of six lines which was wordy and which contained a now less timely allusion to poems on the battle of Blenheim—both by Oxonians—John Philips's *Blenheim* and Addison's *Campaign*.

The occasion was the opening of a season of dramatic performances in Oxford by a group of actors drawn from both London theatres and licensed by the Vice-Chancellor of the University. The place was probably the Tennis Court near Merton College, belonging to Robert à Wood, brother of Anthony, which served at the time as an occasional theatre; the time, June or July; and among the plays performed, Farquhar's latest, *The Recruiting Officer*, Dryden's *Spanish Friar*, and *Sir John Falstaff* (*Henry IV, Pt. 1?*). The audience, we learn from Defoe, writing disapprovingly in the *Review* for 3, 8, 10 August 1706, was composed of the Vice-Chancellor, the heads of houses, and the fellows and graduates— who went to the playhouse in a formal procession—the University students, and the people of the town.

Reprinted with revisions:

> *The Muses Mercury: or Monthly Miscellany Consisting of Poems, Prologues, Songs, Sonnets, Translations, and Other Curious Pieces Never Before Printed* [ed. John Oldmixon], September, 1707, p. 208 (ready 24 October).
>
> Aitken, *Life*, 1889, i. 148.

Text from the *Muses Mercury*, collated with the broadside.

## Prologue to *The Distrest Mother* (*p.* 46)

Ambrose Philips's play, an imitation of Racine's *Andromaque*, was produced at Drury Lane on 17 March 1712 and printed on 28 March (*Spectator* No. 338): The Distrest Mother. A Tragedy. As it is Acted at the Theatre-Royal in *Drury-Lane*. By Her Majesty's Servants. Written by Mr. Philips. Printed for S. Buckley and J. Tonson. 1712. 4to. Steele's prologue was spoken by Robert Wilks, who was not in the cast. Addison and Budgell were responsible for the writing of the epilogue. The play got a great deal of attention from the *Spectator*: it was analysed and praised in No. 290, 1 February 1712 (Steele); the first performance was advertised in No. 328, 17 March (Steele); it was discussed on Sir Roger's attendance, No. 335, 25 March (Addison); the publication was first advertised in No. 338 and the second edition in No. 371, 6 May, with other notices in April and May.

Reprinted:

> *A Collection of the Most Celebrated Prologues Spoken at the Theatres of Drury-Lane and Lincoln's Inn. By a Young Lady.* 1727. 2nd ed. 1728, p. 37.
>
> *Original Prologues, Epilogues, and Other Poems . . . to which is added a*

*Collection of Such as are Celebrated for Wit, Humour or Entertainment*, 1756, p. 39 (an excerpt, in a section titled 'In Praise of Shakespeare').

Aitken, *Life of Steele*, 1889, i. 340 (an excerpt).

Text from the first edition of the play.

## Prologue to *Lucius* (*p.* 47)

A part of this prologue was written to be used at De La Rivière Manley's play, first produced at Drury Lane on 11 May 1717, and was printed with it on 22–25 June (*Evening Post*): Lucius, The First Christian King of Britain. A Tragedy. As it is Acted at the Theatre-Royal in Drury-Lane. By His Majesty's Servants. By Mrs. Manley. Printed for John Barber . . . and sold by Benj. Tooke . . . 1717. The part of Lucius was played by Booth, but there is no record of his having spoken Steele's lines. The epilogue was written by Matthew Prior.

A few years later Steele added fifteen lines, mainly a eulogy of the King, and printed it in his *Theatre* No. 10, 2 February 1720, possibly intending this final form for the author's benefit performance at Drury Lane on 27 April 1720 (*Daily Courant*). For this occasion Wilks was advertised to speak a prologue (*Post Boy*, 21–23 April); but as Steele was not then *persona grata* at the theatre, his probably was not used in either form.

Mrs. Manley dedicated her play to Steele with an expression of gratitude for his endeavour to promote its reputation and success. Her dedication and his prologue marked the end of their long political feud, which had been publicly conducted in paper and pamphlet and was now publicly closed. Her final apology ran as follows:

Be then the very Memory of disagreeable Things forgotten for ever, and give Me leave to Thank you for Your Kindness to this Play, and in return, to shew towards Your Merit the same Good-will.

Reprinted:

(First form) *Lucius*, 2nd ed. corrected. For Barber, Chetwood, and Morphew (*Post Boy*, 2–5 April 1720).

(First form) *A Select Collection of Poems*, ed. Nichols, 1780, iv. 19–20.

Text from *The Theatre*, folio issue, collated with the first form.

## Prologue Intended for the Players at Hampton Court (*p.* 49)

Written in 1718 and printed in Steele's periodical *The Theatre* No. 13, 13 February 1720. The circumstances under which it was composed are related in his letter to the Duke of Newcastle on 21 September 1718. A programme of plays to be performed for the King in the great hall at Hampton Court was to be opened on 23 September with Farquhar's *Beaux'*

*Stratagem*. As Governor of the Drury Lane players Steele in the line of
duty wrote his prologue, which Wilks had memorized, when it became
known that Lord Chamberlain Newcastle had engaged Thomas Tickell
to do the honours. Steele's suggestion that his should be used and that
Tickell's would be suitable for an epilogue was evidently not well taken.
What appears to be the prologue written by Tickell and possibly delivered
on the occasion was printed from unpublished manuscripts by R. E.
Tickell, *Thomas Tickell and the Eighteenth-Century Poets 1685–1740*,
1931, pp. 231–2.

Text from *The Theatre*, folio issue.

## Prologue Intended for *All for Love* Revived (*p.* 50)

First printed together with the prologue for *Lucius* in the *Theatre* No. 10,
2 February 1720, accompanied by Steele's defensive statement, 'to shew
the Town by printing the two following Prologues, that the Governor of
the Theatre bent all his skill and inclination upon serving and celebrating
his Royal Master, who gave him that distinction'. Because of a political
difference with Lord Chamberlain Newcastle, Steele was relieved of his
duties as Governor of Drury Lane early in 1720 and not reinstated until
May 1721.

A corrective statement of the purpose and date of this prologue seems to
be in order. The famous revival of Dryden's tragedy by a distinguished cast
with all new costumes and sets took place at Drury Lane on 3 December
1718 and eight or nine subsequent evenings. A performance was given also
the next season on 17 November 1719 (Genest, ii. 639 and iii. 5). It is
likely that Steele's prologue was written for one of these occasions in 1718
or 1719, possibly that in 1719 which is nearer the climax of the South Sea
Bubble hysteria; for Steele's references to 'funds' and 'stocks' and 'gaming
nights' seem to point unmistakably to this public excitement. Without
doubt he was addressing a London audience in these lines:

> When round pale boards you sit with fiendlike pain
> For base vicissitudes of loss and gain.

Thus the tradition that it was written in 1718 for an amateur performance
of *All for Love* given by young people at Blenheim Palace appears to be
unfounded. The story runs that Steele and Bishop Hoadly were guests of
the Marlboroughs; that both men wrote prologues for the occasion; but
that Steele held his back in deference to the Bishop (*The Theatre*, ed.
Nichols, 1791, pp. 81–82, note). Hoadly's prologue with explanatory
heading is preserved in several eighteenth-century collections.

Reprinted:

*Steele's Epistolary Correspondence*, ed. Nichols, 1809, ii. 473–4.

*Addisoniana*, 1803, ii. 227–9.

Text from *The Theatre*, folio issue.

## Epilogue to the Town Intended to be Spoken in 1721
### (*p. 51*)

A Prologue to the Town, As it was Spoken at the Theatre in *Little Lincoln's-Inn-Fields*. Written by Mr. *Welsted*. With an Epilogue on the same Occasion, by Sir Richard Steele. London. Printed and Sold by J. Brotherton and W. Meadows . . . J. Roberts . . . A. Dodd . . . W. Lewis and J. Graves. 1721. Price 4 Pence. Small folio pamphlet. (Published 3 February, *Daily Post*. Copies at the Folger and the Clarke Memorial Library.)

Neither prologue nor epilogue was spoken. They were intended for a performance of *Measure for Measure* on 23 January 1721 at Lincoln's Inn Fields (*Daily Post*), where Shakespeare's play had been revived in November preceding and several performances given. In his Preface to the pamphlet, Welsted explains that the two poems had been delivered into the hands of the manager John Rich four days before the 23rd and in plenty of time, but to his disappointment had not been used. He had put them into print with Steele's consent. 'A Veteran in this sort of Composition', Welsted called him. What gave birth to the epilogue, he states, was Steele's desire to make another effort to bring the plays of Etheredge into disrepute, particularly *The Man of Mode or Sir Fopling Flutter*: 'Dorimant is the great Giant, the Spoiler, with whom he is at War.' Steele's first attack had been made years before in *Spectator* No. 65, 15 May 1711; and this invective, Welsted explains, was intended to be a 'finishing Stroke'. A point of view contrasting with Steele's, though not specifically related to this epilogue, is to be found in two essays by John Dennis: *A Defence of Sir Foppling Flutter* . . . 1722 (2 November, *Daily Post*) and *Remarks on a Play, Called the Conscious Lovers*, 1723 (25 January).

The epilogue may also be taken as Steele's public congratulation of a rival manager on the successful revival of Shakespeare. It was printed shortly before his reinstatement—following an altercation with the Lord Chamberlain—into the governorship of the Drury Lane Theatre, a position he had held since 1714.

Reprinted:

> *The Works in Verse and Prose of Leonard Welsted Esq.*, ed. John Nichols, 1787, pp. 79–80.

Text from the pamphlet.

## Prologue and Epilogue to *Tamerlane* Revived
### (*pp. 53, 54*)

These poems were written for Nicholas Rowe's tragedy (1702) as performed by schoolboys at Dr. Newcome's School in Clapton, Hackney, probably between 1721 and 1724. They are not to be found in the printed

works of Steele, and there is no allusion to them in the recorded tradition.
Circumstantial evidence, however, in the contents of William Taylor's
commonplace book in which they are found and in *Some Account of the
Taylor Family* (1875), pp. 204–22, leaves no doubt of their authenticity.
The connecting link between Steele and Taylor is their mutual friend,
Bishop Benjamin Hoadly. The sons of Hoadly and Taylor were fellow
students at Dr. Newcome's School in the early 1720's when they were
about the age of Steele's only son Eugene, who died in 1723, aged eleven.
Pathetic evidence is extant in manuscript fragments that Steele wrote pro-
logues for Eugene to deliver at the Censorium, his little theatre in York
Buildings.

Printed by Blanchard, *P.M.L.A.* xlvii. 772–6, September 1932.

Text from the *Manuscript Verse Book of William Taylor*, British Museum,
Add. MSS. 37684, pp. 11, 12.

## Miscellanea (*pp. 57–59*)

### To Benjamin Hoadly, Bishop of Bangor

'Coming home the other night, after your great condescension in liking such
pleasures as I entertained your Lordship with, I made the distich, which
you will find if you turn over the leaf.' (Letter of November 1716[?]
written after a Mug-house entertainment in honour of King William.
See *Correspondence*, 1941, pp. 117–18.)

### To Mrs. Manley

'As for the Verses you quote of mine, they are still my Opinion.'
(Letter of 6 September 1709. See *Correspondence*, 1941, pp. 29, 31.)

### Rhymes in the Plays

*The Funeral*: Act II; *The Lying Lover*: Act I, Act II, Act III; *The
Tender Husband*: Act II, Act III, Act V. i; *The Conscious Lovers*: Act I. ii,
Act II, Act III, Act V; *The School of Action*: Act III.

### Lines for a Poem by Another Hand

The author of the fragmentary poem inserted in the *Tatler* No. 11
(5 May 1709) John Nichols identified as Jabez Hughes (*Tatler*, 1786 ed.,
i. 116). Steele, introducing the verses of his 'kinsman', commended the
liveliness of the image but condemned the rhymes; he explained: 'His lines
are a description of the sun in eclipse, which I know nothing more like than
a brave man in sorrow, who bears it as he should . . . As in the case of

Cato.' Neither the lines by the friend—which follow—or Steele's have been spotted in a printed poem.

Thus when the Ruler of the genial day,
Behind some darkening planet forms his way,
Desponding mortals, with officious care,
The concave drum, and magic brass prepare;
Implore him to sustain the important fight,
And save depending worlds from endless night.
Fondly they hope their labour may avail,
To ease his conflict, and assist his toil.
Whilst he in beams of native splendour bright, ⎫
(Though dark his orb appear to human sight) ⎬
Shines to the gods with more diffusive light. ⎭
To distant stars with equal glory burns,
Inflames their lamps, and feeds their golden urns.
Sure to retain his known superior tract,
And proves the more illustrious by defect.

### Lyric for Italian Music

In his last periodical Steele again decried Italian music as not 'rational' entertainment for an English audience. 'I shall give them a small instance of what is very happily calculated for the service of the present refiners of our taste in Music and Poetry . . . the following Song which is admirably well set to musick by a famous Italian Master . . . it gives no manner of disturbance to the head, but meerly serves to be added to sounds proper for the syllables. . . . The particular words were indeed translated for the Master, and he gave them dying notes accordingly . . . the force, the *pathos* is most admirably laid upon the word *everlastingly*, with a due *impatience* in the notes on *by and by*.' (*Theatre* No. 18, 1 March 1720.)

## Anacreontique to Delia on New-years-day (*p.* 63)

The poem was printed in Charles Gildon's miscellany: Examen Miscellaneum. Consisting of *Verse and Prose*. Of Verse, By . . . the Marquis of *Normandy*. The late Lord *Rochester*. Mr. *Waller*. Mrs. *Wharton*. Mr. *Wolseley*. With Satires and Fables, and Translations from *Anacreon*. In Prose . . . Printed for B.L. and Sold by John Chantry . . . 1702, 8vo., pp. 10–11.

The external evidence for attributing it to Steele is as follows: As his epistle to Congreve was included in Gildon's miscellany of 1701, it is not improbable that the poem by Mr. S—— in the collection of 1702 may also be his. This book we know was at least planned or begun by 15 November 1701, the date when the copy was purchased from Gildon by the publisher, Bernard Lintott (Nichols, *Literary Anecdotes*, viii. 293, 296). And this date may be associated with the facts of a letter Steele wrote to

Colonel Revett on 2 September 1701, which seems to indicate that his thoughts were on literary activities. He was in retirement reading 'two or three excellent authors' and working on his play *The Funeral*, produced in November or December: that is the inference, as he mentions his play and echoes one of the verses used in it. His thoughts were also on his sweetheart Black Moll, referred to as 'Delia'. Therefore it seems possible that the Delia *Anacreontique* was submitted to Gildon about this time as suitable for a miscellany to contain translations of fifteen or sixteen Anacreon odes. Garth, Oldmixon, and William King of the wits were among the unmentioned contributors. It may be significant also that, though Steele was almost invariably referred to as 'Captain' in this period, Gildon had used 'Mr.' in the miscellany of 1701 as it is used here. The volume has no table of contents to afford further clues.

As for the internal evidence, the poem resembles in tone, imagery, and diction the songs of the *Funeral*, which he was then writing. The line 'Tender grief and soft desire' is reminiscent of 'Soft distress and tender woe' in Act II, and 'Behold the future Minutes strive' employs imagery like that in a song of Act IV, 'Ye minutes bring the happy hour'. The word 'Begon' was also on the tip of Steele's pen as is shown from another song in Act IV, 'Begon, thou Meteor'.

Indeed, 'begon' was then a favourite cliché, as indicated, for example, in the *Lying Lover*, v. iii, 'Then doubts and fears . . . begone', and in the *Tender Husband*, IV. i, 'Come, come, no more Instructions . . . be gone, be gone!' Other clichés to be noted are the general terms, 'The Wise, the Grave, the Learned, the Brave', found elsewhere: in the *Funeral* songs, 'the Brave', 'the Fair'; in the *Procession*, 'the Poor, the Brave'; in the prologue of the *Lying Lover*, 'the Learned, the Fair'; in the prologue to the *Distrest Mother*, 'the Wise'; in the *Prologue to the University of Oxford* and the *Verses to Addison*, 'the Learned'.

Repetition of words and phrases was used for two purposes in Steele's verse: for emphasis and for the effect of balance in line or couplet. In the *Anacreontique* striking examples are found of both devices. 'Awake, awake' and 'Begon, begon' are suggestive of the emphatic 'much, much', 'fly, fly', 'take, take', 'arise, arise' in the *Funeral* songs; 'I mourn, I mourn' in a song in the *Tender Husband*; 'for Shame, for Shame' and 'tis time, tis time' in the *Epilogue to the Town*.

An example in the *Anacreontique* of repetition used to secure balance in the couplet is seen in the lines:

> Good Time bestow thy Length of Days:
> Let Length of Days their Portion be,

This is similar to the repetition in the *Verses on Mrs. Selwyn*:

> Thy Wealth and Empire on thy slaves bestow,
> Slaves who no blisse, but Wealth and Empire know.

In the *Procession*:

> Wou'd e'er believe this were *that very Queen*;
> That very Queen, whom Heav'n so lately gave

In the *Prologue to the University of Oxford*:

> Aspiring Columns here, here beauteous Fields,
> Here all that Art, here all that Nature yields,

In a song from the *Tender Husband*:

> *Germania*, give me back my Slain,
> Give me my slaughter'd Sons again.

Or from a Martial epigram:

> Thus through the Glass the lovely Lilly glows,
> Thus through the ambient Gem shines forth the Rose.

In the *Epilogue to the Town*:

> The perjur'd Dorimant the Beaux admire;
> Gay perjur'd Dorimant the Belles desire:

Or from the same piece:

> This is the Tast our sad Experience shews;
> This is the Tast of Belles as well as Beaux:

In the prologue to the *Distrest Mother*:

> A hundred times a crowded Audience drew;
> A hundred times repeated, still 'twas new.

An example in the *Anacreontique* of repetition to secure balance within the single line is seen in this:

> Be those for her, be these for me!

Similarly, we find the device used in the *Prologue to the University of Oxford*:

> Aspiring Columns here, here beauteous Fields,

In the *Lines for a Poem by Another Hand*:

> Alone triumphant, since he falls alone.

In a Martial epigram:

> What Flames, what Darts, what Anguish I endur'd?

A search does not reveal any more plausible candidate for Mr. S——. True George Stepney, whose name is on the title-page, was a contributor to the volume, but his poems are labelled; and in fact there is no similarity between his formal and lifeless verses and this lively bit. It must be mentioned also that a Mr. S—— had contributed two songs to Gildon's *Miscellany Poems* of 1692, but from the context this poet seems to have been 'Mr.' Fleetwood Sheppard, not knighted until 1694.

No reprints of the *Anacreontique* have been found.

## On his Mistress (*p. 63*)

This poem was contributed to the April issue, 1707 (published 31 May), of the *Muses Mercury*, pp. 95–96, a monthly periodical conducted by John Oldmixon to which Steele seems to have pledged his support and which contains three of his signed poems in the January, February, and September issues. The reasons for attributing *On his Mistress* to Steele are (1) the likelihood that other of his poems were included in the periodical, particularly in the early spring issues, (2) the similarity in its subject-matter and treatment to his verse, especially the love poems in the early period. The April issue contains poems assigned to Motteux, Dennis, Mrs. Behn, William Colepeper, Francis Manning, J. H., Sir T. C., S. T., and E. Wolley; *On his Mistress* is one of three unassigned poems. Beginning with this April issue the title-page with a list of the contributors was omitted, and the names or initials of the authors were given in the table and appended to their poems. Steele's name, it must be said, does not appear anywhere.

The question may be asked: if Steele permitted his name to be given with the two frivolous poems in the January and February numbers, why should he prefer to have this one printed without his name in the April number? And there is an answer. By the spring of 1707 he was making every effort to launch himself on a public career, as was Addison, now an under-secretary of state. He left the army at this time and in April or May began his first appointment in government service as editor of the *London Gazette*: light poetry in the vein of love and gallantry doubtless seemed inconsistent with this more serious purpose. His signed *Prologue to the University of Oxford* in the September issue, a sober and dignified poem, however, would in no way compromise Mr. Steele, purveyor of State and war news. Moreover, an editorial note in this September number seems to shed light on his desire for anonymity and sounds, indeed, like his valediction to plays and poetry:

As for Comedies, there's no great Expectation of anything of that kind since Mr. *Farquhar's* Death. The two Gentlemen who would probably always succeed in the *Comick* Vein, Mr. *Congreve* and Capt. *Steel*, having Affairs of much greater Importance to take up their Time and Thoughts (p. 218).

First of all it should be noted that this Delia love poem bears a resemblance in tone and temper to the Delia *Anacreontique* of 1702, which seems pretty certainly to be Steele's. The hall-marks resembling those in his acknowledged poems are the following stylistic details: the triplet, to the use of which he was inclined; the cliché 'mien', repeatedly used in his prose as well as in his verse (for examples in the verse see the *Procession*, the Ode to Marlborough, *Parthenissa*, and the Hampton Court prologue); the word 'Myrtilla', which pleased his fancy, the name 'Myrtle' later chosen for a character in the *Conscious Lovers* and the fictitious editor of his periodical, *The Lover*; the general terms, 'the Bravest and the Wisest', to which he frequently resorted; and the striking use of repetition in the last three lines (examples cited of general terms and repetition in the note above to the Delia *Anacreontique*, pp. 98–100).

A more detailed comment on the *Muses Mercury*, its nature and purpose and Steele's probable connexion with it, will be found in the note to the unassigned poems *Occasion'd upon Sight of Mrs. N——n* and *Prisca's Advice* (pp. 109–11) in the March number, which are scrutinized on the chance that they also are Steele's.

### Prologue Design'd for Mr. D——'s last Play. Written by several Hands (*pp. 66, 68*)
### Love's Relief (*p. 64*)
### To Belinda (*p. 65*)
### To Flavia (*p. 65*)
### On Nicolini's leaving the Stage (*p. 65*)

These unassigned poems were printed in a block together in this order in Steele's *Poetical Miscellanies*, pp. 40–45, and the present editor believes all of them to be by Steele, as chief collaborator in the first. The last three appear to be those singled out also by John Nichols, though his attribution is rather vague: he places them together in his anthology *A Select Collection of Poems*, iv. 74–75, with the note 'Some of these poems, as I have mentioned, I believe to be Mr. Steele's' (referring to a general comment on the anonymity of his poems, iv. 14 n.).

Certain ideas and tricks of expression characteristic of Steele are found in *Love's Relief*. The word 'relief' came easily to mind in various poems: in 'From place to place', where it is likewise associated with love, and in the *Procession* and the prologue to the *Distrest Mother*. The word 'mien' he found useful in both prose and poetry. Another word easy to rhyme was 'severe', found twice as a terminal word in the prologue to the *Lying Lover* and also in the *Procession*. Instances of the use of repetition to secure balance within the line or in the couplet occur here in the first and third stanzas (examples in his acknowledged verse are cited in the note to the *Anacreontique*, p. 98). And the basic idea of the lover emboldened or consoled by wine was one of the conventional themes which he liked and used elsewhere: 'Midnight Bowls' in *To a Young Lady* and 'a lovely bowl' in a rhyme in the *Lying Lover*.

*To Belinda* is an example of the half-serious, half-playful raillery that Steele liked in short poems. *To Flavia* has the mocking tone of several of the early songs; the central idea is similar to the Martial epigram of *Spectator* No. 52; and the oft-used word 'relief' and the repetition in the last line are also significant in the identification of the poem. The three poems:

Reprinted: Nichols, op. cit., 1780 (and not elsewhere).

## On Nicolini's leaving the Stage (*p. 65*)

Printed in Steele's *Miscellanies*, 1714 (published December 1713), and probably written in 1712 about the time of Nicolini's first farewell to London and return to Italy. The attribution is based chiefly on the similarity of the content to the views on Italian music and musicians held and frequently expressed by Steele. Also significant is the fact that its appearance in print was in his own book—in a group of anonymous poems thought to be his—and never elsewhere to the knowledge of the present editor.

Cavalier Nicolino Grimaldi, the great Italian singer, who came to England in 1708, was acclaimed by Steele in *Tatler* No. 115, 3 January 1710, for his excellence as a dramatic performer and by Addison in the *Spectator* for his 'having shewn us Italian music in its perfection'; but both men had their reservations, and there is very little evidence of their having had any personal relations with him. Though Steele admired Nicolini's acting, he was never carried away by his music or his singing; and the ideas of the poem are in harmony with those he expressed elsewhere: distaste for the castrato—'thy emasculating voice'; scorn of the 'idle trills' of the music and the 'nonsense' of the Italian libretto; uneasiness at the popularity of foreign, particularly Italian music, which 'seduces' London audiences, even 'the Wise and the Brave'; nationalistic jealousy of the encroachment of foreigners upon Shakespeare and native drama. An early expression of Steele's disaffection is seen in the epilogue to the *Tender Husband*: 'no more th' *Italian* squaling Tribe admit' who sing in 'Tongues unknown' and are a 'Foreign Insult' to 'this *English* Stage'; and a later expression of it is found in his parody on verses written for Italian music in the *Theatre* No. 18, 1 March 1720. The use of the cliché 'Begon' may be worth noticing and also of the general terms, 'the Wise, the Brave, the Fair'. (See the note for *Anacreontique to Delia*, p. 98.)

For an account of Nicolini's various sojourns in London, see Grove's *Dictionary of Music and Musicians*, vol. iii. That he sang at a concert in London as late in 1712 as 5 April, before leaving, is seen in an advertisement in the *Spectator* No. 335.

Text from *Poetical Miscellanies*, p. 44.

## Prologue Design'd for Mr. D——'s last Play. Written by several Hands (*pp. 66, 68*)

This was written shortly before the revival and benefit performance at Drury Lane on 15 June 1713 of Thomas D'Urfey's comedy *A Fond Husband or the Plotting Sisters*, and was first printed in Steele's *Poetical Miscellanies* in December 1713 (pp. 40–41).

Its authorship has never before—to the knowledge of the present editor—been associated with Steele, but has been generally attributed to Pope. Steele's volume in which its initial and anonymous appearance was made contains three of Pope's poems, two of them not printed before, all labelled plainly as his. Pope did not include it in his collected works of 1717 nor in his 'own' miscellany printed that year. Its inclusion in the Pope–Swift miscellanies of 1727–32 without the by-line 'Written by several Hands' has nevertheless been taken as his indirect acknowledgement of authorship: 'Prologue Design'd for *Mr.* Durfey's last *Play*' (copy examined, 'the last volume', B. Motte, 1727, that is, March 1728, p. 117). On this ground Pope's modern editors have printed it or listed it with his known writings, usually without any reservations—an attribution somewhat puzzling in view of the contrast between the sympathetic tone of the prologue and Pope's consistently contemptuous, if good-natured, comments on D'Urfey and his songs and plays (passages from 1710 to 1728 cited by James Sutherland, *The Dunciad*, 1943, p. 439). Its authorship seems never to have been called in question by responsible editors (printed in Elwin-Courthope, *Works*, 1882, iv. 416; listed by Griffith in *Bibliography*, 1922, i. 287, as 'Composed by Pope and others'; credited to Pope by Sutherland, op. cit., p. 439 and by Ault, *New Light on Pope*, 1949, p. 136; printed as Pope's by D'Urfey's editor, Cyrus L. Day, *The Songs . . .*, 1933, pp. 23–24). Possibly the only critics to question Pope's authorship spoke in malice, shortly after the prologue's appearance in the Pope–Swift miscellanies in 1728, accusing plagiarism: 'the *Prologue* to Mr. *Durfey*'s last Play was written at *Button's* in a publick Room, *by several hands*' (a citation from *The London Evening-Post*, 4 April 1728, quoted in *A Compleat Collection of all the Verses, Essays, Letters and Advertisements, which have been occasioned by the Publication of Three Volumes of Miscellanies by Pope and Company*, 1728, p. 23).

In the first place it seems reasonable to accept Steele's by-line for what it says and to believe that pretty certainly Addison, possibly Pope, who was then friendly with the Addison–Steele circle, and possibly others were among the collaborators. But the most clearly discernible hand is Steele's. The main project—to give countenance to D'Urfey's benefit performance of his play *A Fond Husband or the Plotting Sisters*—must be credited to both Addison and Steele; the character, spirit, and ideas of the prologue designed to be spoken at the theatre at the time or printed then are demonstrably Steele's.

On 28 May 1713 in *Guardian* No. 67 Addison spoke in a friendly way of his intervention at the playhouse on behalf of D'Urfey, who was 'reduced to great difficulties'; announced the forthcoming revival and benefit on 15 June; and bespoke the patronage of the town. Who in the summer of 1713 would have more influence at Drury Lane than the author of *Cato*? Then on the day of the performance in *Guardian* No. 82, Steele in the role of sponsor wrote at length of the author, play, production, and actors and urged the public 'to make an honest man a visit of two merry hours to make his following year unpainful'. Whether the prologue was spoken is not known; but there can be no doubt that this was the play for which it was intended, because it was the 'last play' of D'Urfey's performed before the publication of Steele's *Poetical Miscellanies* in December 1713, where the prologue appeared.

Two other of D'Urfey's plays were sponsored by Steele: the first performance of *The Modern Prophets* in May 1709, and also its publication, and the revival of *The Richmond Heiress* in June 1714 (see Genest, *Some Account of the English Stage*, ii. 418, 527). Moreover, during a period of almost ten years in his various periodicals, giving D'Urfey the benefit of whatever prestige he may have had with the public, Steele spoke out for the 'ancient Lyrick' (*Tatler* Nos. 1, 4, 11, 43, 214, 1709–10; *Guardian* No. 82, possibly also No. 29, 1713; *Lover* No. 40, 1714; *Theatre* No. 18, 1720). The story that he followed D'Urfey to his grave in 1723 and was bequeathed his gold watch cannot be verified, but there may be truth in it. Although the tone of Steele's championship may be described as jocular, it is unmistakably warm, kindly—and appreciative. Indifferent to the conventional attitude of the wits, who regarded D'Urfey as a perennial joke, but not unaware of it, he always spoke of him as 'my friend Mr. Thomas D'Urfey', 'my old friend', 'my honored friend', 'my ingenious friend'. It was also 'my friend and his writings', 'the judicious author', 'the man of extensive genius': his respect for D'Urfey's contribution to theatrical entertainment in two fields—the song and the light farcical play—was genuine. D'Urfey was not in the mode, possibly never had been, but the originality of his genius, particularly in song-writing, Steele appraised with critical acumen:

[*The Modern Prophets*] the 25th Production of my Honour'd Friend Mr. Thomas D'Urfey, who, besides his great Abilities in the Dramatic, has a peculiar Talent in the Lyrick Way of Writing, and that with a Manner wholly new and unknown to the Antient *Greeks* and *Romans*, and is but faintly imitated in the Translations of the Modern *Italian* Opera's (*Tatler* No. 1, 12 April 1709).

The last phrase of the statement is a crux, one suspects, in Steele's appreciation of D'Urfey—his songs were of native origin.

And he regarded the ageing D'Urfey as a gallant old trouper who had 'diverted many Generations in the Theatre . . . in the Character of a Poet' and still possessed ability to give the town 'two merry hours'. To Steele the social values of his songs and plays may possibly have seemed of greater importance than the aesthetic: he had been 'wonderfully useful to the World'. Undoubtedly he also felt humane sympathy for the man in his needy old age.

These then are Steele's ideas, all to be found in the prologue: the public indebtedness to D'Urfey for his long service in theatrical entertainment:

Grown Old in Rhyme, 'twere barbarous to discard
Your persevering, unexhausted Bard:

His present crying need for patronage:

Tho' Plays for Honour in old Time he made,
'Tis now for better Reasons—to be Paid.

His two gifts—for song-writing and comedy:

> 'Tho *Tom* the Poet writ with Ease and Pleasure,
> The Comick *Tom* abounds in other Treasure.

His originality and independence of the classical tradition:

> He scorn'd to borrow from the Wits of Yore;
> But ever Writ as none e'er Writ before.

> .      .      .

> And little would be left you, I'm afraid,
> If all your Debts to *Greece* and *Rome* were paid.

The lines are witty but not ironical. It is conceivable that Pope, whose prologue for *Cato* had been so recently acclaimed, did have a hand with others at Button's in fashioning some of the verses or polishing them, that he was proud of his participation, that he had a copy at hand when he made up the miscellanies in 1727–8, and that after correcting one redundant line he printed the prologue without the by-line—to the confusion of his editors. But the evidence certainly points to Steele as the prime mover; and the prologue as a whole—its underlying spirit, its tone, its ideas, and its wit—suggests not Pope but Steele. In the opinion of the present editor, tradition and custom to the contrary, it should be placed with Steele's writings. As far as we can ever know his hand was the chief among 'several'.

Reprinted by Nichols, *A Select Collection of Poems*, 1780, iv. 99.
Text from Steele's *Poetical Miscellanies*.

## Prologue at the Opening of the Theatre-Royal, the Day after His Majesty's Publick Entry. Spoken by Mr. Wilks (*p.* 68)

This prologue was printed by Tonson on 24 September 1714 on a single folio sheet ('this day', *Daily Courant*; listed by Morgan, *A Bibliography of British History 1700–1715*, 1937, ii. 511) and was reprinted in the second (i.e. third) edition of Steele's *Poetical Miscellanies*, 1727, pp. 309–10. The occasion for its delivery was the first night of the theatrical season, 21 September 1714, when Farquhar's *Recruiting Officer* was played at Drury Lane (Genest, ii. 547). The King had landed at Greenwich on the 18th and on the 20th had made his first royal entry into London (Oldmixon, *History*, 1735, p. 572). It can be safely attributed to Steele on the basis of internal evidence, but external facts also support the assumption that it is his.

Though a single detail in the poem characteristic of Steele's thought and expression could not be regarded as conclusive evidence of his authorship, the group of them taken together carry conviction: the allusion to *Cato* and other stage productions as incitement to zeal for the Hanoverian cause; the nationalistic bias expressed against France; the mention of the value of tears as catharsis—'Lest you . . . forget to Weep'; the use of the ever-present cliché 'generous' (compare 'generous' pity, love, passions, mind, &c., in other poems); the repetitive design 'How did', &c., near the beginning; and the idea in the last couplet which Steele used conspicuously in other prologues, for example:

'Tis what our Sovereign feels . . .
Which gives her glorious Cause such high Success,
That only on the Stage you see Distress. (Epilogue to the *Lying Lover*, 1703.)

Rescu'd from foreign Bonds, the happy Age
Sees no Abuse of Power, but on the Stage:

On such dire Forms, long shall this happy Isle,
As only Stage-Events in Safety Smile; (Prologue to *Lucius*, 1717.)

Corroborative evidence is found in external facts. For two years past Steele had not spared himself in journalistic activities in the cause of the Revolution Settlement and the Protestant Succession—as he once earnestly said, 'a Cause in which I am engaged to the end of my Life'; and it would be strange if an expression of his loyalty were not found among the numbers of poems in 1714 on the King's entry, accession, and coronation. That it would be a prologue for use at Drury Lane Theatre might be forecast—and that Tonson would publish it. Anonymity would be expected.

A new appointment for the governorship of Drury Lane was in order upon the Queen's death in August, and Steele had the wheels moving at once, we learn from his letter to Mrs. Steele on 8 September. The position was secured through the influence of the Duke and Duchess of Marlborough, but a note in the Steele papers at Blenheim indicates the direct interest of the King himself: 'Message from the King to know whether I was in earnest in desiring the Playhouse or that others thought of it for me—If I lik^d it I should have it as an earnest of his future favour.' His licence is dated 18 October 1714. This prologue must have had its place in the sequence of happenings.

Undoubtedly there is significance in its inclusion in the 1727 edition of the *Poetical Miscellanies*. But, as Steele was ill and living in retirement in Wales, it was probably Tonson or his deputy who made the selection of the dozen or so poems added to the first edition. A number of these are pieces for which he had the copyright, for example, Tickell's *A Poem on the Prospect of Peace*, Prior's [?] *Epistle from the Elector of Bavaria to the French King* . . ., and Addison's *To her Royal Highness the Princess of Wales* . . . and *To Sir Godfrey Kneller, on his Picture of the King*. Like the prologue several, Addison's among them, are without the author's name.

Reprinted:
Nichols, *A Select Collection of Poems*, iv. 96–97. 'From Steele's Miscellanies.'

Text from the 1727 edition (the folio not seen by the present editor).

## Prologue Spoken at the Sensorium on His Majesty's Birth-day (*p.* 69)

This prologue was printed in No. 7, 27 January 1716, of *Town-Talk* with a reference to No. 4, 6 January, where Steele described the occasion on which it was spoken. This was an entertainment that he gave at his little theatre in Villars Street, York Buildings, on 28 May 1715, in honour of the King's anniversary. The prologue was 'very prettily spoken' by Miss Elizabeth Younger. No clue is given in either paper as to its author, and it has not been attributed heretofore to Steele. The strong probability is, however, that none other was responsible for it. He would certainly have desired to welcome his guests in his own way and to take the opportunity to set forth the purpose of his current project the 'Censorium', which was well exemplified in the entertainment of this particular evening. The description he gave of it in No. 4 tallies so closely with the details in the prologue that it would be difficult to think of the two as having been written by different hands. 'Music, Eloquence, and Poetry' were to constitute the programme (compare the passage beginning 'To you shall Bards their Virgin-Works reveal') 'with representations of some great incidents in antiquity in the manner in which they were transacted' (compare the lines beginning 'The *Grecian* Gesture, and the *Roman* Tone'). The guests were 'one hundred ladies and one hundred gentlemen of leading taste in politics, art and learning' (compare 'An Audience rather Elegant than Great', &c.) and their seating arrangement in the hall—'the ladies and gentlemen oppositely disposed . . . the seats for the audience amphitheatrically built' (compare 'While Wit and Beauty shall the Scene divide . . . rang'd on either Side').

The mention of 'the Neighb'ring Barge-men' in the prologue may be a reference to Actor Doggett's celebration on the same occasion, the sponsoring of a competitive boat-race for the watermen from London Bridge to Vauxhall, in the vicinity of the scene of the Censorium. At any rate in No. 4 containing the description of his own programme Steele gave also an account of Doggett's 'on May last . . . and the noisy huzzas of the watermen', &c.

The general tone of the prologue and its style suggest Steele's hand. One stylistic detail should be especially noticed: the word *treat* in the third line was one of his clichés for prologues, used similarly in the prologue to the *Distrest Mother* (1712) and that to *Lucius* (1717). This Censorium prologue was attributed to Thomas Tickell in a newspaper account of the entertainment, *Weekly Packet* for 28 May–4 June 1715, but it has never since been connected with his name in his works or elsewhere. Except in Nichols's editions of *Town-Talk*, 1789, and 1790, it has not been reprinted since Steele's time until now.

Text from *Town-Talk*, original issue.

# POEMS OF
# DOUBTFUL AUTHORSHIP

There is no decisive evidence for attributing to Steele the poems listed below. But because in subject-matter or treatment they suggest his hand or because they are printed in places or in circumstances that raise the question of his authorship, it seems desirable to review them in this study of his verse. The gulf that lies between possibility and certainty either way a reader of the book may be able to span.

## Occasion'd upon Sight of Mrs. N——n
## Prisca's Advice to Novinda

There is only a slight possibility that these poems printed in the March number of the *Muses Mercury*, 1707 (published 24 April), were written by Steele, but the facts should be reviewed here. John Oldmixon's monthly periodical ran from January 1707 to January 1708. In his Introduction to the first number Oldmixon stated that it was designed to be a literary paper akin to the *Gentleman's Journal* of the 1690's, its province to be 'ev'ry Thing that has any relation to the Studies of Humanity': it would print poetry, prose essays, and dramatic criticism and would give news of books, current plays, and operas; nothing in it would be injurious to 'good Sense and good Manners'. It was undertaken, he said, with the help of friends who had supplied him with 'a Stock to set up with'; and others interested were invited to offer contributions. A desire for anonymity would be respected. Steele would have approved such a project heartily, and apparently he was one of those who consented to support Oldmixon, as his name appeared on the title-page of the first three issues—thereafter the title-page was discontinued; and his signed poems were included in the January, February, and September issues.

The names printed on the title-pages of the January and February issues were Roscommon, Dryden, Garth, Tate, Dennis, Dr. Henry Newton, Francis Manning, and Captain Steele. For the March issue two names, Dr. Newton and Manning, were withdrawn and two were added, Mrs. Behn and W. W., Esq.; but Steele's name remained. This March issue contained nine or ten poems by persons not mentioned on the title-page, and there was nothing in it by Tate, Dryden, Garth, or Dennis. It is quite possible, of course, that Oldmixon was holding Steele's verse in reserve for later issues, as he apparently was holding Garth's and Dennis's. But, suspecting that at this time Steele desired anonymity for his light verse,

one should at least scrutinize the five anonymous pieces in the March issue
for a possible contribution from his pen. (His reasons for desiring anonymity
are discussed in the note to *On his Mistress*, p. 101.)

The two poems, *Occasion'd upon Sight of Mrs. N——n* (pp. 58–59) and
*Prisca's Advice to Novinda* (pp. 59–60) must be considered together, for
an editorial note states that they were by the same hand:

> The two following Poems, particularly that of *Prisca's Advice to Novinda*,
> will no doubt be very acceptable to Readers, and especially to the Ladies. The
> Author, whose Merit is very well known, seems to imitate Mr. *Waller's* manner
> both in the Numbers and the Turn . . . (p. 58).

*Occasion'd* is a poem of twenty-four lines in octosyllabic metre with alternat-
ing rhyme, beginning:

> Is this the wondrous matchless Fair,
> Whose new-discover'd Charms conspire,

The idea developed is that it is only because Mrs. N——n is a toast that
she attracts more attention than the many other British women as beautiful
as she: lacking 'the pow'rful *KitCats* mark', even 'Beauty must not current
prove'. The poem was printed in May of the same year (*History of the
Works of the Learned* for May) in The Poetical Works of Sir *Charles
Sedley* . . . with a New Miscellany of Poems by Several of the most
*Eminent Hands*. For Sam. Briscoe and B. Bragg, 1707, pp. 207–8. Here
it follows *The Play-House*, 'By J. Addison, Esq.,' and has the by-line, 'By
another Hand'. In this form it is lengthened to twenty-eight lines, revised
in several places, and printed in four-line stanzas; and the lady is called
simply Mrs. N——. It should be noted here, perhaps, that a Mrs. Nicholas
was a toast of the club in 1703 (*Verses Written for the Toasting-Glasses of
the Kit-Kat Club in the Year 1703*: these lines attributed to Dr. B——).
Although Steele as a member of the Kit-Cat Club had doubtless done his
share of publicizing Whig beauties, there would be no particular reason to
suspect his touch in *Occasion'd* were it not attached to the other.

*Prisca's Advice* 'By the same Hand' consists of twenty-four lines in
couplet beginning

> Trust not false Man, th' experienc'd *Prisca* cries,
> Think on my Fate, and Oh! be timely wise.

The theme is that of the disillusioned older woman warning another,
young and inexperienced, of the vanities of the *beau monde*.

## Prisca's Advice to Novinda (revised and lengthened)
## Novinda's Answer to Prisca

Two years after its appearance in the *Muses Mercury, Prisca's Advice* in a
lengthened form of fifty-eight lines was printed in the Dryden–Tonson
miscellany, 1709, Part VI. 537–41 (published on 2 May, *London Gazette*

of 28 April). This time it was accompanied by a companion piece, *Novinda's Answer* (pp. 541–4), a poem of sixty lines in pentameter couplet, beginning:

> When Gen'rous *Prisca's* early Counsel came,
> I frown'd to read, and scarce forbore to blame,

The second piece serves to present the central idea more fully and to press home the moral: 'When Conduct fails, how tott'ring is the Throne.'

There is no decisive evidence for attributing these poems to Steele. They are considered here in connexion with doubtful poems for the reasons that in theme and treatment they resemble pieces which he admired; that they are included in a book in which he was known to have had a special interest; and that they are printed there in close company with two other poems which also raise the question of his authorship.

We know that Steele found attractive the general idea of one woman discussing with another the subject of feminine weaknesses and follies. Rochester's poem on this theme, *A Letter from Artemisa in the Town to Cloe in the Country*, made such an impression upon him that he quoted from it again and again (see Introduction, *infra*). To cite only one other instance, Lady Winchilsea's *A Pastoral Dialogue between Two Shepherdesses*, printed in this same Dryden–Tonson volume, elicited from him an expression of admiration (in *Tatler* No. 10, 3 May 1709).

From a statement made in a letter to Mrs. Steele on 5 February 1709 the inference has been drawn that Steele was a member of the committee to choose the poems and translations to be included in this sixth and last part of the Dryden–Tonson miscellany:

> ... am indispensably obliged to dine at Tonson's where after dinner some papers are to be read whereof, among others, I am to be a Judge.

And his comment in *Tatler* No. 10, immediately after its appearance, seems to indicate special interest in its reception. Nicholas Rowe, thought to have been chosen by Tonson to be editor of this volume (see *Books Printed for E. Curll*, 1735, p. 14), was a friendly acquaintance; and the poets represented in it were, many of them, his friends—Pope, Philips, Rowe, Swift, Garth, Harrison, Eusden, Tickell, and Hughes. And it seems not unlikely that Steele himself would make a contribution, though perhaps anonymously. He had, of course, been represented in poetical collections in 1707 and 1708. It may or may not be significant, but the fact should be considered that these two poems are printed in proximity with two occasional poems, also anonymous, which conceivably he may have written: *On the Countess of Br——wt——r's Recovery* and *To the Queen; upon the Death of His Royal Highness*. The possibility must not be overlooked, however, that none of the four was written by Steele but that, appealing to his taste and interest, all of them might have been merely his choice for inclusion in the volume.

Reprinted in collected editions of the miscellany in 1716 and 1727.

### On The Countess of B——wt——r's Recovery

This was printed in the Dryden–Tonson miscellany, 1709, vi. pp. 536–7. It has sixteen lines and begins:

> The Gods at first, in Pity to our Race,
> Grieving to view the Triumphs of her Face,

The subject of the poem was Lady Elizabeth, Countess of Bridgwater (1687–1714), the daughter of the Duke of Marlborough, and the wife of Scroop Egerton, fourth Earl of Bridgwater, afterwards Duke, to whom she had been married in 1703. From the year of her marriage she had been one of Queen Anne's ladies of the bedchamber and hence something of a public figure. She seems to have been a striking personality known for her kindly charm and lovable personality. In 1703 she was toasted by the Kit-Cats in the verses of Arthur Maynwaring, and later Pope paid his tribute to her beauty in his *Epistle to Jervas*. No record exists of Steele's having known the beautiful young lady, but there would seem to be no doubt of his acquaintance at least with her husband because of their association in the household of Anne's consort, Prince George of Denmark. Steele held the minor post of Gentleman-Waiter from 1706 to 1708; Bridgwater was one of the Commissioners of the Prince's Revenue and at the time of the Prince's death in October 1708 was Master of the Horse. The official duties of the two men on some occasions might conceivably have brought them together. It is perhaps unnecessary to mention in this connexion Steele's almost idolatrous devotion to Lady Bridgwater's father.

No account has been found of the illness which would furnish a clue to the date of the poem's composition; but a guess might be the birth of the daughter Lady Anne in 1707 or 1708.

The tone of the panegyric is suggestive of Steele; and certain tricks of expression are similar to his, for example, the use of repetition for emphasis: 'She lives, She lives!' (see the note to the Delia *Anacreontic*, p. 98); and the use of the favourite word 'Doom' and of the word 'relief' to rhyme with 'grief' as in the funeral poem for Queen Mary, in the prologue to the *Distrest Mother*, and in 'From place to place'.

Reprinted in the collected editions of 1716 and 1727.

### To the Queen; upon the Death of His Royal Highness

Included in the sixth and last volume of the Dryden–Tonson miscellany, 1709, p. 547. It is a poem of thirty lines; opening couplet:

> Whilst Tears o'erflow the Royal Widow's Bed,
> And gloomy Sadness veils her Sacred Head;

As Gentleman-Waiter to Prince George of Denmark, the Queen's consort, from 1706 to 1708, Steele would be likely to write such a poem upon the

Prince's death in 1708; and the content, tone, and diction are not unlike his thought and expression. He had mournful duties from the day of the Prince's death at Kensington Palace on 28 October until the funeral in the Abbey on 13 November. These are referred to in a series of letters to Mrs. Steele on 28, 29 October and 12, 13 November:

I came hither [he tells her] according to my Duty to attend the Prince My Master, by whose Dead Body I sitt while I am writing this.

Could it have been during one of these lonely vigils—'every third night till He is interred'—that the poem was conceived and written?

Touches suggestive of Steele's verse-writing can be detected. An epistle of warm personal sympathy addressed to the Queen rather than a formal panegyric of the colourless Prince might be expected of him. The sombre tone appropriate in a funeral poem is accentuated by an emotional ardour which is also characteristic: 'Sympathetic Anguish', Publick Tears', 'Compassion', 'Soft Embrace', 'tend'rest Part', 'Paradise of Love'. The didactic tenor in the thought is arresting, as are the presence of words and phrases that recur in Steele's writing. The word 'relief' is found again—here as in the *Procession*, the prologue to the *Distrest Mother*, and the song in the *Conscious Lovers* to rhyme with 'grief'; 'just Motive' and 'asswage' were clichés of his; and 'Conscious looks' is particularly tell-tale—compare 'conscious' honour, majesty, eyes, gust, goodness, innocence, and love in other poems.

A dozen or more funeral poems were written on this occasion, several appearing as separate publications. Of the anonymous ones examined by the present editor none has any similarity to Steele's known verse. A poem not traced, however, with a similar title, written by one Charles Dive, *Gent.* and published by Morphew, was advertised for the period between November 1708 and February 1709 (*Term Catalogues*, ed. Arber, iii. 621). But whether or not a separate publication of Morphew's would be used in Tonson's book is a question.

Reprinted in the collected editions of 1716 and 1727.

## To a Lady on her Parrot

Opening line, 'When Nymphs were coy, and Love could not prevail'. Five couplets printed in a *Tatler* paper by Steele, No. 27, 11 June 1709, in the section dated 'Will's Coffee House'. An enlarged and more indelicate version entitled *Myra's Parrot* was included in *Poems upon Several Occasions* by George Granville, Lord Lansdowne, 1712, p. 45, but does not appear in his definitive edition, *The Genuine Works in Verse and Prose*, 2 vols., 1732. The *Tatler* version was printed also in *The Festival of Love*, 1789, p. 29.

## A Song

A poem of three four-line stanzas beginning 'Belinda, see from yonder flowers' found in one of Steele's *Spectator* papers No. 473, 2 September 1712. The correspondent, who signs himself 'Timothy Stanza', writes: 'You professed authors are a little severe upon us, who write like gentlemen. But if you are a friend to love, you'll insert my poem. . . . My crime was that I snatched a kiss, and my poetical excuse as follows.' A musical setting for it by William Hayes is found in *Twelve Arietts or Ballads and two Cantatas*, Oxford, 1735, No. 9, 'The Words Taken out of the Spectator'.

## From Anacreon
### Ἄγε ζωγράφων ἄριστε

Opening line: 'Best and happiest Artizan'. A translation of Ode No. XXVIII (so numbered in Bullen's edition, 1893), *To a Painter: How to Paint His Beloved*, consisting of thirty-six lines in octosyllabic couplet. It appeared in *Guardian* No. 168, 23 September 1713, for which Steele was undoubtedly responsible, purporting to come from an unnamed correspondent. Several times during the course of the century it was reprinted but with no identification except 'From the Guardian'.

Reprinted:

> John Addison, *The Works of Anacreon*, 1735, pp. 99–101.
> Francis Fawkes, *The Works of Anacreon*, 1760, pp. 69–72.
> *The Festival of Love*, 1789, p. 140.

## A Song

Opening line 'Tell me, Miranda, why should I' of a poem of four four-line stanzas appearing in an unsigned letter in Steele's periodical *The Lover* No. 35, 15 May 1714. The correspondent expressed views on courtship similar to those held by Steele: 'I am one of those unfortunate Men, who think young Women ought to be treated like Rational Creatures. I forbear therefore to launch out into all the usual Excesses of Flattery and Romance. . . . If she sees you think these [verses] tolerable enough to allow them a Place in your Paper, I am in hopes they may help to hasten the Happy Day.'

## An Ode to Freedom

A poem of seven four-line stanzas beginning 'Freedom! Goddess frank and fair', which is given in *Town-Talk* No. 4, 6 January 1716, a paper by Steele, describing the Censorium entertainment on 28 May 1715. It is described as 'an Ode which was admirably performed in honor of the King and Royal Family and addressed to the person seated on the Throne in the habit and ensigns of Liberty'. No mention is made of the author. A poem by Leonard Welsted similar in design, entitled *Ode for the Prince's Birthday* (published 14 January 1716), that Steele said was written at his request and was intended to be spoken at the Censorium on the Prince's Birthday, was included in another *Town-Talk* paper, No. 9.

## To Serena: on presenting her *The Conscious Lovers*, Written by Sir Richard Steele

A poem of twenty-one lines, pentameter couplets and a triplet, with the opening line—'If e'er thou should'st the dang'rous Passion prove'. It is included in Miscellaneous Poems, by Several Hands: Particularly the D—— of W——n, Sir Samuel Garth, Dean S——, Mr. John Hughes, Mr. Thomson, Mrs. C——R. Publish'd by Mr. *Ralph.* 1729. pp. 212–13. Dedication signed J.[ames] Ralph.

The phrase 'Written by Sir Richard Steele' refers more than likely to the authorship of the play. It could be argued, however, that the sentimental tone, the ideas, the diction, and the phrasing sound like Steele. The clichés 'gen'rous Mind', 'gen'rous Soul', are his; and 'None of her Grief, but all her tender Joy' is an echo of a song in the *Funeral*, 'None of thy Grief but all thy Joy'. As the poem is addressed to a very young girl, another argument for Steele's authorship could be that it was intended for his daughter Elizabeth, aged fourteen in 1723 when the play was printed. We know that he inscribed other books for her as she was growing up: for example, a copy of Welsted's *Epistles, Odes, &c.*, is extant which he presented to her on 20 March 1723[-4] (advertised by Messrs. Maggs in *Mercurius Britannicus* No. 119, February 1950). It has not been established whether the editor of the collection, James Ralph, was the 'J.R.' who in 1721 dedicated to Steele the second volume of *The Antiquities of St. Peter's or the Abbey-Church of Westminster.*

## Epitaph on Tom D'Urfey

Three couplets beginning:

> Here lyes the *Lyrick,* who with Tale and Song
> Did Life to threescore Years and ten prolong:

It is found in Miscellaneous Poems by Several Hands. Published by *D. Lewis,* 1726 (p. 6), which also contains David Lewis's epistle: *To Sir Richard Steele. On his Comedy, The Conscious Lovers* (pp. 66–68). Steele genuinely respected 'that ancient Lyrick, Mr. *D'Urfey*' (*Tatler* No. 214) for his contribution to stage entertainment. According to one tradition D'Urfey left his watch to Steele, who is said to have arranged and paid for his burial in the porch of St. James, Piccadilly. An inscription was placed on the south side of the church: 'Tom Durfey. Dyed Feb^ry ye 26: 1723.' For a summary of their relations, see the note to *Prologue Design'd for Mr. D——'s last Play* (pp. 103–106).

# LOST POEMS NOT FOUND

## A Recorded Prologue not Found: To the Town, 1720

A farce 'never before acted' entitled *The Theatre*, 'all in the characters of the Italian Theatre', was performed at Lincoln's Inn Fields on 22 and 23 April 1720 with 'a Prologue by Steele'. So reads the record of the annalist (Genest, *Some Account of the English Stage*, 1832, iii. 43). Further information can be gleaned from advertisements in the *Daily Post* of 22 and 23 April. It was a short play, only one item in a miscellaneous bill, and the prologue was addressed 'to the Town': 'a new Farce of two Acts, call'd *The Theatre*. . . . With a new Prologue to the Town by Sir Richard Steele . . .'. There is no reason to doubt that such a prologue was written for the Lincoln's Inn Fields Theatre. At this particular time Steele was smarting under the withdrawal of his licence as Governor at Drury Lane; and we are certain of at least one epilogue he submitted to Rich in January 1721 for performance at the rival theatre (see *infra*, p. 96). No trace of the prologue has been found, however, and the farce which it was intended to introduce has never been identified.

It is only a conjecture, ventured by the present editor with hesitation and with little supporting evidence, that the short farce published in 1727 and attributed on the title-page to Thomas D'Urfey, who had died in 1723, may answer to the description of Genest: *The English Stage Italianiz'd in a New Dramatic Entertainment Called Dido and Aeneas: or Harlequin. A Butler, a Pimp, a Minister of State, Generalissimo, and Lord High Admiral; dead and alive again, and at last crown'd King of Carthage by Dido. A Tragi-Comedy, after the Italian Manner by Way of Essay, or first step towards the farther Improvement of the English Stage. Written by Thomas D'Urfey. Poet Laureat de Jure.* For A. Moore, 1727. (Copy examined at the Huntington Library.) The satire is very crude, and it is difficult to believe that Steele would have any part in entertainment so gross; but it is a fact that he would have been in hearty agreement with the germ of this idea—satire on foreign stage customs, especially Italian music and opera, which he considered harmful to the English theatre. This nationalistic bias had pervaded his thinking and writing for many years; and even in March, a month before the farce was performed, he was decrying Italian music in his current periodical *The Theatre* No. 18, 1 March. If the author of this farce was indeed D'Urfey—the attribution is questioned by his editors—this fact would be another motive for the participation of Steele, who had long been his admirer and his champion, as the aged poet had found it increasingly difficult to interest the public in his plays. Steele's goodwill is shown in *Tatler*, *Guardian*, and *Lover* papers (see pp. 103ff.), and it may be significant in this connexion that he seems to be pleading

D'Urfey's cause, if unostentatiously, in the *Theatre* shortly before the date of prologue and farce; the motto for No. 9, 30 January is the following quotation and translation:

> *Tu contra audentior ito*—Virgil [*Aeneid*, 6. 95]
>
> For Fate still will have
> A Kind Chance for the Brave
>     D'Urfey's Translation [folio issue].

Steele's periodical, designed as a vindication and defence of the English stage, came to an end on 5 April 1720; had it continued through the month, the lost prologue, like several other of his prologues, might be found in its pages. (I am indebted to Professor John Loftis for calling my attention to the Genest and *Daily Post* records of this lost prologue.)

## Fragments of Projected Prologues

The source of all these fragments is the collection of Steele papers known as the Blenheim MSS., some of which are still preserved at Blenheim Palace and others of which were sold at Messrs. Sotheby's in July 1920.

(1) Autograph jottings on scraps of paper labelled 'Prologues for York Buildings' contain such hints as the following:

> A poor Decrepid built this costly Dome
> To bring . . .
> The World he cannot visit to his Home
>
> The ——? of the Alphabet Agree
>
> Dryden, Cowley, the King's health
> By Cowley's Labour
> The King's health only if it is his own wishing
>
> Here at one Glance . . .

(2) What seems to be the working draft of a piece designed for a specific occasion is headed 'Prologue' and consists of seventeen or eighteen lines beginning:

> Hats uncockt not to frighten the Audience
> Not to intimidate the Audience. . . .

This one-page autograph manuscript was advertised by Messrs. Maggs Brothers, London, in *Catalogue* No. 497, 1927, Item No. 2558, with a facsimile reproduction, Plate XXIII.

(3) The fragment of a prologue beginning:

> A Cunning Cripple rais'd
> This little Theatre, this Nations[?] gaudy Dome

(Transcribed by John Loftis. See 'Richard Steele's Censorium', *Huntington Library Quarterly*, Nov. 1950, p. 65.)

(4) A projected prologue for Steele's unfinished comedy *The School of Action*:

Minutes for the play itself. . . . For the Prologue take notice of this play as a *Posthumous Work* according to Dr. Partridge's friends. Spider and Dottrell's Quality—Beasts made before men—Therefore the Dottrells must give way, for they were made before Spiders were in being. . . .

Autograph notes printed with the unfinished play by Aitken, *Richard Steele*: Mermaid Series, 1894, pp. 363–4.

# POEMS WRONGLY
# ATTRIBUTED TO STEELE

## Two Lapland Love Songs

'Thou rising Sun, whose gladsome Ray' in *Spectator* No. 366, 30 April
  1712 (Steele).
'Haste, my Rain-Deer, and let us nimbly go' in *Spectator* No. 406,
  16 June 1712 (Steele).

These poems were contributed to the *Spectator* by two different correspon-
dents, the first in No. 366 having been identified as Ambrose Philips (by
Henry Morley[?] see Aitken's *Spectator*, v. 249 n.). They are described in
Steele's editorial introductions to the letters as translations or adaptations
of Lapland love songs given in Professor John Scheffer's *History of Lapland*,
a Latin work of 1673, which had had English editions in 1674 and 1704.
In that of 1674 (pp. 112–15) the songs are given both in the 'Lapland
tongue' and in a rough poetical translation. All during the century the
*Spectator* versions were popular and frequently turned up in collections of
songs, 'Thou rising Sun' with musical settings by Dr. Arne, Christopher
Smith the younger, William Richardson, 'Mr.' Digard, William Hayes,
and William Boyce. In these collections uncertainty as to their authorship
is expressed, or they are attributed to the *Spectator*, Addison, or Steele.
Joseph Ritson, who spoke on the subject with something like authority,
attributed them tentatively to Sir Richard Steele in the first edition of his
work, *A Select Collection of English Songs*, 1783, i. 216, 223; in the second,
however, he wavered between Steele and Addison (1813, i. 252).

Ambrose Philips's interest in Scandinavian literature is credible. His
poem entitled *Winter Piece* and dated 'Copenhagen, March 9, 1709', was
written while he was serving as secretary to Daniel Pulteney, Envoy to
Denmark. Steele had printed it on 7 May in the *Tatler* No. 12. Nothing
is said of Philips's authorship of either Lapland song in his collected poems,
1937.

## The Croxall 'Spencer Poems'

An Original Canto of Spencer: Design'd as part of his Faery Queen, but
  never printed. Now made publick. By Nestor Ironside, Esq., 1714.
  (Published late November 1713). Second edition, 1714 (early
  December).
Another Original Canto of Spencer. . . . Now made publick. By Nestor
  Ironside. 1714.

Samuel Croxall wrote these poems and printed them under the pseudonym
of Nestor Ironside, who was the fictitious editor of Steele's *Guardian*, only

recently in October having come to a close. The subject-matter was a political allegory, displeasing to the Tories, and Steele was attacked in the *Examiner* of 14–18 December 1713 on the assumption that he was the author. Though their authorship was shortly disclosed, the 'Spencer poems' are still to be found occasionally under Steele's name in book lists and library catalogues.

## EPILOGUE
### Spoken at the Censorium on the King's Birth-Day.

Opening lines:

> The Sage, whose Guests you are to-Night, is known
> To watch the Public Weal, tho' not his own;

Thirty-four lines of pentameter couplets. This is a playfully satiric account of Steele's numerous and hopeful projects 'for his Country's Good', from the alchemy experiments of his youth up to the forthcoming Hoadly–Steele anti-papist tract 'to convert the Pope', couched in deft and pointed couplets. It was spoken by Robert Wilks at Steele's entertainment at the Censorium on 28 May 1715 and was first printed, with no mention of the author's name, in his periodical *Town-Talk* No. 4, 6 January 1716.

It has been attributed to both Steele and Addison. The present editor is of the opinion that Addison was responsible for it. It does not appear in Tickell's edition of Addison's *Works* in 1721, but was first reprinted and attributed to Addison by John Nichols in *A Select Collection of Poems*, 1782 (viii. 263). Since then Addison's editors including Bohn, 1862 (vi. 532), and Guthkelch, 1914 (i. 186–7), have generally regarded it as his. Steele's biographer Aitken also attributes it to Addison, 1889 (ii. 60). On the other hand, from his own day to this, various writers have believed it Steele's. A newspaper account of the entertainment at the time in *Weekly Packet*, 28 May–4 June 1715, states explicitly that 'the epilogue was written by himself which was very merry and free with his own Character'; and a pamphlet of 1720, *The Crisis of Honesty*, hostile throughout, refers to it as 'a kind of Prologue you made upon yourself' (p. 22). John Nichols in the course of his reading and thinking apparently changed his mind and reversed his judgement, naming Steele as the author in *Epistolary Correspondence*, 1809 (ii. 382). Others ascribing it to Steele are the editor of *Addisoniana*, 1803 (ii. 250–2); Nathan Drake, *Essays*, 1805 (i. 124–5); and the biographer Connely, 1934 (p. 293), who regarded it as Steele's joke upon himself.

It is true that the wry, deprecatory self-analysis of the epilogue sounds somewhat like Steele. But the main argument for his authorship seems to have been the *Weekly Packet* account written by a reporter who was able to supply circumstantial details. Some of these are accurate, but others, for example, the attribution of the prologue for the occasion to Tickell, in the opinion of the present editor are unreliable. Also doubtful is the emphasis on the lavish arrangements—'pyramids of all manner of Sweetmeats, the most generous Wines, as Burgundy, Champaign etc.'—an emphasis that seems to have annoyed Steele who, in commenting on the reasonable expense of the entertainment, says that 'it was much below what some with a kind and others with a malicious design reported it'.

Perhaps the chief argument against Steele's authorship lies in the couplets themselves, precise, concrete, sententious and, it must be admitted, unlike his loose, general, and frequently inflated style. Moreover, a close reading of *Town-Talk* No. 4 reveals self-consciousness in what he has to say about 'that celebrated epilogue'. Despite the urbaneness of his comment on the 'sanguine temper' so 'admirably rallied' in the epilogue, one detects in it a defensive or hurt tone:

the undertaker of the Censorium, who is a comic hero, or familiar sage, seems to expect success in his great enterprizes by being and bearing anything with his friends while they are such, and abating and remitting nothing to his enemies till they cease to be so. Were not this his turn of mind, it would have been impossible for him to have stood the loud laughter, on the several occasions, wherein Wilks made no scruple of pointing at him, while he spoke the Verses I am now going to recite.

That Addison had similarly rallied Steele on his projects in *Guardian* No. 107, 14 July 1713, may not be of any significance in this connexion; but a small clue in *Town-Talk* (which is addressed to a lady in the country) is arresting. At the end of No. 4 immediately following the printed epilogue is a statement that seems to be a hint that all during the discussion of the epilogue he has been thinking of Addison and invites the reader also to do so: 'P.S. I send you all the *Freeholders* that are come out; they are very Entertaining, Honest and Instructive.' Addison's periodical ran from December 1715 to June 1716. In 1715 and the early part of 1716 Steele and Addison were still on friendly terms. But very soon thereafter the old closeness of the two men gave way to a separateness and coolness which eventually became an estrangement.

To the present editor it seems altogether probable that what happened was that for his first (and only?) programme at the Censorium Steele him-himself wrote the prologue and invited Addison to write the epilogue.

Reprinted by Nichols, Drake, Bohn, Guthkelch, Aitken as stated above.

## Prologue to *The Conscious Lovers*

A Prologue to the Conscious Lovers [by Sir R. Steele]. Spoken the 7th of March, 1722[3]. By the Ghost of Sir Fopling Flutter. On Occasion of its Being Play'd at the Request of the Young Gentlemen of the College, Dublin. Dublin, 1723. Folio half sheet.

Opening lines:

> Ladies, ye stare as if ye knew me not—
> What! Can Sir *Fopling* be so soon forgot?

The prologue described above is attributed to Steele and printed as his by Joseph Wood Krutch in *Comedy and Conscience after the Restoration*, 1924, pp. 245–6; as far as the present writer knows, the attribution has not been made elsewhere. Steele's name is probably not given on the printed half-sheet, the name on the entry in the *Catalogue of the British Museum* (as stated above) referring to the authorship of the *Conscious Lovers*. The author of the prologue may possibly have been Matthew Concanen or one of the contributors to his miscellany, where it is printed anonymously, together with several other prologues spoken at the Theatre Royal in Dublin: *Miscellaneous* Poems, Original and Translated, By Several Hands. Viz. Dean Swift, Mr. Parnel, Dr. Delany, Mr. Brown, Mr. Ward, Mr. Sterling, Mr. Concanen, and Others. Published by Mr. *Concanen*. London: 1724, p. 220. The tone of the poem can hardly be interpreted as ironical; and as satire the content is so extremely derisive of the moralist Steele and his reforming play that it is impossible to believe it came from his pen. Other poems in the volume also make fun of him.

It seems that Steele did not himself write prologue or epilogue for the *Conscious Lovers*; with the printed play we find a prologue and an epilogue by Leonard Welsted, the latter with the heading 'Intended to be spoken by Indiana', i.e. Mrs. Oldfield. Just what happened at the first performance is not on record, but an epilogue was in print on 2 December 1722, about the same time as the play, with the explanatory heading: 'The Epilogue to the *Conscious Lovers* as spoken by Mrs. Oldfield, but omitted in the printed Play.' This one is probably by Benjamin Victor, as it is prefixed to the second edition of his *Epistle to Sir Richard Steele, on his Play Called the Conscious Lovers* (*Daily Journal*). The opening lines are:

> Now, I presume, our moralizing Knight,
> Is heartily convinc'd my Sense was right.

Two anonymous epilogues were printed separately in Dublin for performances given there in March 1723 and May 1724, but there is no reason to believe that either was written by Steele.

## A Poem on the Irish Harp

Orpheus Redivivus: A Poem on the Irish Harp, with an Encomium on the Famous Mr. Morphy's Performance thereon. By Sir Richard Steel. Corke: Printed by A. Welsh. [1723.]. Printed in red on a single folio sheet.
   The opening lines:

> By Learned Antiquarians we are told
> The Harp was Modish in the Times of Old.

That this is spurious there can be little doubt, though Steele may have heard the famous Irish harpist, John Murphy, and expressed an 'encomium' on his playing. An anonymous letter to Steele is extant dated 26 March

1723 informing him of the publication of the broadside, 'this day': 'ye Enclosed Copy of Verses on his performances, under too great name for Such poetry wʰ I think but justice to acquaint you of' (*Correspondence*, 1941, p. 179). The present editor has not seen the broadside, which is described in *Catalogue* No. 457, 1924, of Messrs. Maggs Brothers, London. Its provenience was the Blenheim MSS.

# INDEX OF FIRST LINES

A wretch long tortur'd with disdain . . . . . 64
Against a woman's wit, 'tis full as low . . . . . 57
All the commanding powers that awe mankind. . . . 41
And woman's happiness, for all her scorn . . . . 57
Arise, arise great dead for arms renown'd . . . . 20
As wand'ring streams by secret force return . . . . 45
At length, Britannia, rescu'd from thy fears . . . . 68
Awake, awake, bright nymph appear . . . . . 63

Begon, our nation's pleasure and reproach . . . . 65
Belinda, see from yonder flowers . . . . . . 114
Best and happiest artizan . . . . . . . 114
Bright dames when first we meet unheeded passe . . . 35
Britons, who constant war, with factious rage . . . . 42
By learned antiquarians we are told . . . . . 122
By what power did she enslave me . . . . . 35

Cynderaxa kind and good . . . . . . . 19

For bright assemblies, and for tastes refin'd . . . . 69
For since through all the race of man we find . . . . 57
Freedom! Goddess frank and fair . . . . . . 114
From place to place forlorn I go . . . . . . 26

Grown old in rhyme, 'twere barbarous to discard . . . 66

Haste, my rain-deer, and let us nimbly go . . . . 119
Hats uncockt not to frighten the audience . . . . 117
Here lyes the Lyrick, who with tale and song . . . . 115
How hard t'will be to go to school again . . . . 54
Howe'er we're wont to feign, we now appear . . . . 49

If e'er thou should'st the dang'rous passion prove . . . 115
In church the prayer-book, and the fan display'd . . . 65
Is this the wondrous matchless fair . . . . . 110

Ladies, ye stare as if ye knew me not . . . . . 121
Let not love on me bestow . . . . . . . 19
Let Rufus weep, rejoice, stand, sit, or walk . . . . 34
Love, hope and fear, desire, aversion, rage . . . . 40

Me Cupid made a happy slave . . . . . . 33
Must I then passive stand! and can I hear . . . . 11

Nat. Lee—for buskins fam'd—would often say . . . 47
Nature's deserted and dramatick art . . . . . 39
Now, I presume, our moralizing knight . . . . . 122

Old Horace says, a man who us'd t'expose . . . . 53
On yonder bed supinely laid . . . . . . 20
One minute, Fortune, thou hast let me live . . . . 32
Our author's wit and raillery to-night . . . . . 43
Our too advent'rous author soar'd to-night . . . . 41

See, Britons, see with awful eyes . . . . . . 23
Shou'd Addison's immortal verse . . . . . . 14
Since Cælia cou'd, to love unjust . . . . . . 32
Since faint is praise, which living merit draws . . . . 50
Since fancy of it self is loose and vain . . . . . 46
Since the day of poor man . . . . . . . 22
So notwithstanding heretofore . . . . . . 59

Tell me, Miranda, why should I . . . . . . 114
The days of man are doom'd to pain and strife . . . 3
The gods at first, in pity to our race . . . . . 112
The rolling years the joys restore . . . . . . 22
The sage, whose guests you are to-night, is known . . . 120
There needs not time true passion to discover . . . . 58
They may be false who languish and complain . . . . 58
They only who gain minds, true lawrels wear . . . . 58
Thou rising Sun, whose gladsome ray . . . . . 119
Thou soft machine that do'st her hand obey . . . . 21
'Tis not the lover's merit wins the field . . . . . 57
To hope for perfect happiness is vain . . . . . 58
Trust not false man, th' experienc'd Prisca cries . . . 110
Truth is too simple, of all art bereav'd . . . . . 58

Venus has left her Grecian Isles . . . . . . 21
Virtue with so much ease on Bangor sits . . . . 57

We use all arts the fair to undermine . . . . . 57
What could our young dramatic monarch mean . . . 51
Whate'er the generous mind it self denies . . . . 58
When all the globe to Caesar's fortune bow'd . . . . 58
When Arria pull'd the dagger from her side . . . . 33
When gen'rous Prisca's early counsel came . . . . 111

When my bright consort, now nor wife nor maid . . . 35
When nymphs were coy, and love could not prevail . . . 113
When pleasure's falling to the low delight . . . . 12
When the three charming beauties of the skies . . . . 63
While gentle Parthenissa walks . . . . . 26
While in a lovely bowl I drown my care . . . . 57
While you the fierce divided Britons awe . . . . 15
Whilst in the dark on thy soft hand I hung . . . . 34
Whilst in the grove Timandra walks . . . . . 86
Whilst tears o'erflow the royal widow's bed . . . . 112
Why, Belvidera, tell me why . . . . . . 84
Why lovely charmer, tell me why . . . . . 25
With secret impulse thus do streams return . . . . 14
With studied airs, and practis'd smiles . . . . . 25
Would you reform an heedless guilty age . . . . 58

Ye fair, whose charms on chrystall records rise . . . . 90
Ye minutes bring the happy hour . . . . . 19

# GENERAL INDEX

*Account of the State of the Roman Catholick Religion, An, see* Steele.

Addison, John, *The Works of Anacreon*, 114.

Addison, Joseph, xiv, xix, xxiv, 11, 15, 75, 76, 90, 92, 101, 103, 104, 119; *The Campaign*, xiv, 45, 79, 93; *Prologue to The Tender Husband*, 92; *The Play-House*, 110; *Epilogue to The Distrest Mother*, 93; *Cato*, 15, 79, 104, 106; *To her Royal Highness. . . ,* 107; *To Sir Godfrey Kneller. . . ,* 107; *The Freeholder*, 121; *Epilogue Spoken at the Censorium*, 120–1.

*Addisoniana*, xxii, 95, 120.

Aikin, John, *Essays on Song-Writing*, 81, 88; *Vocal Poetry*, 81, 85, 88.

Aitken, George A., xxii, 75, 76, 88, 119; *Life of Richard Steele*, 75, 76, 78, 79, 80, 81, 83, 86, 88, 93, 94, 120; *Richard Steele*: Mermaid Series, 118.

*Allusion to Horace: Satire I. 10* (Rochester).

*Amaryllis*, 85.

Anacreon, 98, 99, 114.

*Anacreontique to Delia on New-year's day*, xvi, 63, 98–100, 102, 103.

Anderson, Robert, *The Works of the British Poets*, xxi.

Anne, Queen of England, 14, 42, 107, 112, 113.

*Another Original Canto of Spencer* (Croxall).

*Antiquities of St. Peter's or the Abbey-Church of Westminster, The*, 115.

*Apollo's Cabinet or the Muses Delight*, 85.

Arne, Thomas, 84, 86, 119; *Songs in the Comedies Called As You Like It and Twelfth Night*, 85.

*Artful Mistress, The*, 84.

Ault, Norman, *New Light on Pope*, 104.

5402      K

*Aviary, The*, 81, 82, 83, 85, 86, 88.

Ayloffe, William, 77.

B, Dr., 110.

Bagley, Mr., 86.

Barrett, John, 84.

*Bashful Virgin, The*, 88.

*Bayle's Dictionary*, 75.

Beard, John, 87.

*Bee, The. A Collection of Choice Poems.* Part II, xx, 75.

Behn, Aphra, 101, 109.

Bennet, Thomas, 73.

*Biographia Britannica*, xxii.

Bishop, Thomas, *To Captain S. on His Poetry*, xxii.

Blackmore, Sir Richard, *Prince Arthur*, 76; *King Arthur*, 76; *Satyr against Wit*, 75, 76, 78; *Discommendatory Verses*, 76.

*Blenheim* (J. Philips).

Blenheim MSS., xx, 88, 90, 107, 117, 123.

Boas, F. S., *Songs and Lyrics from the English Playbook*, 82, 85.

Bohn, H. G., 79, 120.

*Book of English Songs, The*, 85.

Booth, Barton, 43, 92, 94.

Boston Public Library, 83, 85, 87, 88.

Bowen, James, 20, 80.

Boyce, William, 119.

Boyer, Abel, *Letters of Wit, Politicks and Morality*, xx, 77.

Boys, Richard C., *Sir Richard Blackmore and the Wits*, 76.

Bradley, Arthur, 85.

Bridgwater, Lady Anne, 112.

Bridgwater, Elizabeth Churchill, Countess of, 112.

Bridgwater, Scroop Egerton, Earl of, 112.

Brown, Thomas, xx, 75, 112, 122; *Commendatory Verses*, 75, 76; *Works*, 76.

Buckingham and Normandy, John
  Sheffield, Duke of, 98.
*Buck's Bottle Companion, The*, 88.
Budgell, Eustace, xix, 93.
Bullen, A. H., 114.
Bullock, William, 82.
Burnaby, William, 77.
Burney, Charles, *History of Music*, 86.
Butler, Samuel, xv.
Button's Coffee House, 104, 106.
Byng, George, Viscount Torrington,
  50.

C., Sir T., 101.
*Calliope or English Harmony*, 87, 88.
Campbell, Kathleen W., *Poems on
  Several Occasions. Written in the
  Eighteenth Century*, 89.
Campion, Mary Ann, 80, 81.
Carroll, Mrs., *see* Centlivre.
Case, A. E., *A Bibliography of English
  Poetical Miscellanies 1521-1750*, 74.
*Catalogue of Manuscript Music in the
  British Museum, The*, 88.
Censorium (or Sensorium) in Villars
  Street, York Buildings, 97, 108,
  114, 120.
Centlivre, Susannah, 77, 115.
*Charmer, The*, 81.
*Charming Sounds: a Volume of Early
  Eighteenth-Century Songs* (Greville).
*Chearful Glee, A* (J. S. Smith).
Cheek, Thomas, 77.
Chetham Library, Manchester, Broad-
  sides: No. 94, 92; No. 1489, 87.
*Choice, The*, 81, 83, 84, 85, 86, 88.
*Christian Hero, The, see* Steele.
Cibber, Colley, 91.
Cibber, Theophilus, *Lives of the
  Poets, The*, xxii.
Clive, Mrs. Catherine, 84, 85.
Codrington, Christopher, xxii, 75.
Colepeper, William, 101.
*Collection of Bacchanalian Songs, A*, 83.
*Collection of English Songs, A*, 85.
*Collection of Epigrams, A* (Oldys).
*Collection of Poems, A* (Dodsley).
*Collection of Poems, A* (Pearch).
*Collection of Select Epigrams, A*
  (Hackett).

*Collection of Songs by Mr. Richard
  Leveridge, A* (Leveridge).
*Collection of Songs of Various Kinds
  and for Different Voices, A* (J. S.
  Smith).
*Collection of Songs with the Musick by
  Mr. Leveridge, A* (Leveridge).
*Collection of the Choicest Songs and
  Dialogues, A*, 80, 81.
*Collection of the Most Celebrated Pro-
  logues, A*, 93.
Collier, Jeremy, *A Short View of the
  Immorality and Profaneness of the
  English Stage*, 77.
*Commendatory Verses on the Author of
  the Two Arthurs* (Brown).
*Compleat Collection of all the Verses,
  Essays . . . occasioned by the Publica-
  tion of Three Volumes . . . by Pope
  and Company, A*, 104.
*Complete Collection of Old and New
  Songs, A*, 82.
Concanen, Matthew, *Miscellaneous
  Poems, Original and Translated*,
  122.
Congreve, William, xiv, xvi, xvii, xix,
  76–78, 101; *On Mrs. Arabella
  Hunt Singing*, 12; *The Mourning
  Muse of Alexis*, 12; *The Mourning
  Bride*, 13; *The Way of the World*,
  12, 76–78; *Doris*, xvii; *Works*, 77.
Connely, Willard, *Sir Richard Steele*,
  120.
*Conscious Lovers, The, see* Steele.
Corneille, Pierre, *Le Menteur*, 82.
Cotes, Digby, 79.
Cowley, Abraham, 117; *Of Greatness*,
  xv; *Of Obscurity*, xv; *The Waiting-
  Maid*, xv; *On the Death of Sir
  Anthony Vandike*, xv.
*Crisis of Honesty, The . . . In a Letter to
  Sir R—— S——*, 74, 120.
Croft, William, 80, 81, 82.
Cross, Thomas, 87.
Croxall, Samuel, *Original Canto of
  Spencer, An*, 119; *Another Original
  Canto of Spencer*, 119.
*Cupid, The*, 81, 85, 88.
Curll, Edmund, *Books Printed for*, 111.
Cutts, John, Lord, xviii, 73.

*Daily Courant*, 83, 86, 92, 94, 106.

Dalton, Charles, *English Army Lists and Commission Registers 1661–1714*, 88.

Davies, Thomas, *Miscellaneous and Fugitive Pieces*, xxi.

Day, Cyrus L., *The Songs of Thomas D'Urfey*, 104.

Defoe, Daniel, *The Review*, 93.

Delany, Patrick, 122.

*Delightful Pocket Companion for the German Flute, The*, 86.

Denham, Sir John, *Cooper's Hill*, xv; *The Destruction of Troy*, xv.

Dennis, John, xviii, 87, 89, 101, 109; *A Defence of Sir Foppling Flutter*, 96; *Remarks on a Play Called the Conscious Lovers*, 87, 96; *The Critical Works*, 87.

Derby, Elizabeth Butler, Countess of, 6, 74.

Digard, Mr., 119.

*Discommendatory Verses* (Blackmore).

*Distrest Mother, The* (Philips).

Dive, Charles, 113.

*Diverting Post, The*, 78, 79.

Dobson, Austin, xxii, 75; *Richard Steele*, 75, 78, 91.

Dodsley, Robert, *A Collection of Poems*, xxi.

Doggett, Thomas, 108.

Donne, John, xv.

Drake, Nathan, *Essays, Biographical, Critical, and Historical*, 75, 87, 120.

Drury Lane Theatre, 79, 80, 83, 86, 93, 94, 95, 104, 107, 116.

Dryden, John, xiii, xv, 50, 76, 89, 109, 117; writer of prologues, xiii; *All for Love*, 50, 95; *The Spanish Friar*, 93.

Dryden–Tonson *Miscellany*, Collected editions, 1716, 1727, 111, 112. See *Poetical Miscellanies: the Sixth Part*.

Duncombe, William, *The Works of Horace in English Verse*, 79.

D'Urfey, Thomas, xx, 66, 79, 103–6, 115; *Wit and Mirth or Pills to Purge Melancholy*, xx, 79, 80; *A Fond Husband*, 103–4; *The Modern Prophets*, 105; *The Rich-mond Heiress*, 105; *Songs Compleat, Pleasant and Divertive*, 79, 80; *The English Stage Italianiz'd*, 116; *The Songs of*, 104.

Ellis, Welbore, 14, 78.

Elwin and Courthope (editors of Pope), 104.

*English Stage Italianized in a New Dramatic Entertainment, The* (D'Urfey).

*Englishman, The*, see Steele.

*Epigrams of Martial, The*, 90.

*Epilogue Spoken at the Censorium on the King's Birth-Day*, 120–1.

*Epilogue to The Conscious Lovers* (Victor).

*Epilogue to The Funeral*, 40–41, 91.

*Epilogue to The Lying Lover*, 41–42, 91.

*Epilogue to The Tender Husband*, 42–43, 91, 103.

*Epilogue to the Town*, xx, 51, 96, 99, 100.

*Epistle from the Elector of Bavaria to the French King*, 107.

*Epistle to Sir Richard Steele, on His Play Called the Conscious Lovers* (Victor).

*Epitaph on Tom D'Urfey*, 115.

*Essays, Biographical, Critical and Historical* (Drake).

*Essays on Song-Writing with a Collection of Such English Songs . . .* (Aikin).

Estcourt, Richard, 42, 91.

Etheredge, Sir George, *The Man of Mode or Sir Fopling Flutter*, 52, 96.

Eusden, Laurence, xiv, xix, 79, 111.

*Examen Miscellaneum* (Gildon).

*Examiner, The*, 120.


*Fair Kitchen-maid, The*, 81.

Farquhar, George, 77, 101; *The Recruiting Officer*, 93, 106; *The Beaux' Stratagem*, 95.

Fawkes, Francis, *The Works of Anacreon*, 114.

Fenton, Elijah, xx, xxii; *Oxford and Cambridge Miscellany Poems*, 79.

*Festival of Love, The*, 113.

*Festoon, The. A Collection of Epigrams* (Graves).

Flatman, Thomas, xv.

Folger Library, 76, 79, 80, 81, 86, 96.

*From Anacreon. To a Painter: How to Paint His Beloved,* 114.

*Funeral, The, see* Steele.

G, Mr., 77.

Galliard, John Ernest, 26, 86, 87.

Garrick, David, xiii.

Garth, Dr. Samuel, xiv, 11, 75, 77, 79, 89, 99, 109, 111, 115.

Gay, John, xiv, xix.

Geminiani, Francesco, 85, 87.

Genest, John, *Some Account of the English Stage,* 95, 105, 106, 116.

*Gentleman's Journal* (Motteux).

George I, King of England, 48, 68, 69, 94, 95, 106–7, 108, 114, 117, 120.

George, Prince Consort of Queen Anne, 86, 112.

Gildon, Charles, xx, 76–77; *Miscellany Poems upon Several Occasions,* 100; *A New Collection of Poems,* xx, 76; *A New Miscellany of Original Poems,* xx, 76; *Examen Miscellaneum,* 98.

Granville, George, *see* Lansdowne.

Graves, Richard, *The Festoon. A Collection of Epigrams,* 90.

Greene, Maurice, 84, 87.

Greville, Ursula, *Charming Sounds: A Volume of Early Eighteenth-Century Songs,* 88.

Griffith, R. H., *Alexander Pope: A Bibliography,* 104.

Grove, Sir George, *Dictionary of Music and Musicians,* 103.

*Guardian, The, see* Steele.

Guthkelch, A. C., 120.

H., J., 101.

Hackett, John, *A Collection of Select Epigrams,* 81.

Halliwell-Phillipps, James, 92.

Harding, W. N. H., 81, 83.

Harris, Mrs., 80.

Harrison, William, xiv, xix, 111.

Hay, William, *Select Epigrams of Martial,* 90.

Hayes, William, *Twelve Arietts or Ballads and Two Cantatas,* 114.

Haymarket Theatre, 92.

*Historical MSS. Commission,* 90.

*History of the Works of the Learned, The,* 92, 110.

*Hive, The,* 81, 82, 83, 84, 85, 86, 88.

Hoadly, Dr. Benjamin, 57, 95, 97, 120.

Hogarth, William, 83.

Hooker, Edward N., *The Critical Works of John Dennis,* 87.

Hopkinson, Francis, 86.

Houghton Library, 82, 84, 85, 86, 87.

Howard, Samuel, 86, 87.

Hughes, Francis ( ?), 84.

Hughes, Jabez, 97.

Hughes, John, xiv, 79, 85, 111, 115.

Hunt, Mrs. Arabella, 12.

Huntington Library, 73, 116, 118.

*Imitation of the Sixth Ode of Horace Apply'd to the Duke of Marlborough, An,* xxii, 14, 78, 101.

*Indiana's Song in The Conscious Lovers,* xvii, 26, 86–88.

*Irresistable Charmer, The,* 86.

Italian music, satires on, 42, 59, 65, 86, 116.

Jacob, Giles, *Poetical Register,* xxii.

Jeffreys, George, xix, 79.

Johnson, Dr. Samuel, xxi.

King, William, 99.

Kit-Cat Club, 35, 90, 110, 112.

Krutch, Joseph Wood, *Comedy and Conscience after the Restoration,* 122.

Lansdowne, George Granville, Lord, 76, 77; *Poems upon Several Occasions,* 113; *Genuine Works in Verse and Prose,* 113.

*Lapland Love Songs,* 119.

*Lark, The,* 81.

Lee, Nathaniel, 47.

*Letter from Artemisa in the Town to Cloe in the Country, A* (Rochester).

Letters of Wit, Politicks, and Morality (Boyer).

Leveridge, Richard, 20, 22, 82, 83; A Collection of Songs by . . . , 83; A Collection of Songs with the Musick by . . . , 83.

Lewis, David, Miscellaneous Poems by Several Hands, 115; To Sir Richard Steele. On his Comedy, the Conscious Lovers, 115.

Life a Bubble, 83.

Life Improved, 83.

Lincoln's Inn Fields Theatre, 76, 96, 116.

Lines for a Poem by Another Hand, 58, 97, 100.

Linnet, The (Orpheus I), 81, 88.

Lintott, Bernard, 79, 82, 92, 98.

Loftis, John, 117, 118.

London Gazette, The, 74, 76, 101, 110.

London Magazine, The, 85.

London Songster or Polite Musical Companion, The, 82.

Lover, The, see Steele.

Love's Relief, 64–65, 102.

Lowe, Thomas, 87.

Lucius, First Christian King of Britain (Manley).

Luttrell, Narcissus, 73.

Lying Lover, The, see Steele.

Lyric for Italian Music, 59, 98.

Maggs, Messrs., of London, 115, 117, 123.

Man of Mode, The (Etheredge).

Manley, Mrs. de la Rivière, 47, 57, 97; Lucius, First Christian King of Britain, 47, 94, 95.

Manning, Francis, 89, 101, 109.

Marlborough, John Churchill, Duke of, xvi, 14, 79, 95, 107, 112.

Martial, xx, 33–35, 89–90, 100, 102.

Martin, Benjamin, Miscellaneous Correspondence, 86.

Mary II, Queen of England, 3, 4, 6, 8, 73, 74.

Mase, Owen, 88.

Masque, The, 82.

Mattocks, Master, 87.

Maynwaring, Arthur, 112.

Merry Musician or a Cure for the Spleen, The, 83.

Milton, John, Paradise Lost, xv.

Miscellanea (Steele), 57–59, 97–98.

Miscellaneous and Fugitive Pieces (Davies).

Miscellaneous Poems by Several Hands (Lewis).

Miscellaneous Poems by Several Hands (Ralph).

Miscellaneous Poems, Original and Translated (Concanen).

Miscellanies (1728–32) (Pope and Swift).

Miscellany Poems upon Several Occasions (Gildon).

Monro, George, 87, 88.

Monthly Masks of Vocal Musick, The, xx, 82, 83, 84, 85.

Monthly Miscellany or Memoirs for the Curious, xxi.

Morgan, W. T., A Bibliography of British History, 1700–1715, 106.

Morley, Henry, 119.

Morphew, John, 94, 113.

Motteux, Peter, Gentleman's Journal, xxi, 109; Epilogue, 92.

Murphy, John, 122.

Muses Mercury, The (Oldmixon).

Musical Companion, The, 85, 88.

Musical Miscellany, The, 84, 85, 87, 88.

Myra's Parrot, 113.

N, Mrs., 110.

N——n, Mrs., 110.

New Collection of Poems on Several Occasions, A (Gildon).

New Foundling Hospital for Wit, The, xxi.

New Miscellany of Original Poems, A (Gildon).

New Song, A, 85.

Newberry, John, 85.

Newcastle, Thomas Pelham-Holles, Duke of, 94, 95, 96.

Newcome, Dr., 96, 97.

Newton, Dr. Henry, 89, 109.

Nicholas, Mrs., 110.

Nichols, John, xxi, xxii, xxiii, 78, 95, 97, 120; *Literary Anecdotes*, 98; *A Select Collection of Poems*, xxii, 75, 78, 79, 90, 94, 102, 106, 107, 120; *The Works of Leonard Welsted*, 96; *The Epistolary Correspondence of Sir Richard Steele*, 79, 89, 90, 95, 120.
Nicolini (Nicolino Grimaldi), 65, 103.
*Nightingale, The*, 88.
*Nonplus, The*, 85.
Norris, Henry, 82.
*Notes and Queries*, xxii.
*Novinda's Answer to Prisca*, 110–11.
Nutt, John, 79.

*Occasion'd upon Sight of Mrs. N——n*, 89, 102, 109, 110.
*Ode for the Prince's Birthday* (Welsted).
*Ode to Freedom, An*, 114.
*Odes and Satyrs of Horace*, xx, 79.
Oldfield, Anne, 122.
Oldham, John, xv.
Oldmixon, John, xx, 77, 89, 99; *The Muses Mercury*, xx, 92, 93, 101, 109; *History of England*, 106.
Oldys, William, 89, 90.
*On his Mistress*, 63, 101, 109.
*On Nicolini's leaving the Stage*, xvii, 65, 102, 103.
*On The Countess of B——wt——r's Recovery*, 111, 112.
*Original Canto of Spencer, An* (Croxall).
*Original Prologues, Epilogues, and Other Pieces*, 92, 93.
Ormonde, James Butler, Second Duke of, 4, 73, 74, 88.
*Orpheus Redivivus*, 122–3.
*Oxford and Cambridge Miscellany Poems* (Fenton).

*Painful Part of Love Renounc'd, The*, 81.
Parnell, Thomas, xix, 122.
*Pastoral Dialogue between Two Shepherdesses, A* (Winchilsea).
Pate, Mr., 20, 80.
Pearch, George, *A Collection of Poems*, xxi.
Pepusch, J. C., 85, 87.

Philips, Ambrose, xiv, xix, 79, 111; *A Winter Piece*, 119; *The Distrest Mother*, 43, 93.
Philips, John, *Blenheim*, 45, 93.
Pinkethman, William, 80, 82.
Playford, Henry, xx; *The Diverting Post*, xx, 78, 79.
*Poem on the Irish Harp, A*, 122.
*Poems on Several Occasions. Written in the Eighteenth Century* (Campbell).
*Poems upon Several Occasions* (Lansdowne).
*Poetical Farrago*, 90.
*Poetical Miscellanies, Consisting of Original Poems and Translations* (Steele).
*Poetical Miscellanies: the Sixth Part. Containing a Collection of Original Poems. With Several New Translations* (Dryden–Tonson), xvi, xviii, xx, 110, 111, 112.
*Poetical Register* (Jacob).
*Poetical Works of Sir Charles Sedley, The* (1707), 110.
Pope, Alexander, xiv, xvi, xix, 104–6, 111, 112; *Prologue to Cato*, 79, 106; *Epistle to Jervas*, 112; *The Pope–Swift Miscellanies* (1728–32), 74, 104, 106.
Porter, George (conspirator), 11.
*Post Boy*, 76, 79, 80, 94.
*Post Man*, 77, 82, 84.
Prior, Matthew, xiv, 94, 107.
*Prisca's Advice to Novinda*, 109, 110.
*Procession, The*, xviii, xix, xx, xxii, 3, 73, 100, 101.
*Prologue and Epilogue to Tamerlane Revived*, 53–54, 96.
*Prologue at the Opening of the Theatre-Royal the Day after His Majesty's Publick Entry*, xx, 68–69, 106.
*Prologue design'd for Lucius King of Britain*, 47, 94, 95, 107, 108.
*Prologue Design'd for Mr. D——'s Last Play. Written by Several Hands*, 66–68, 102, 103, 115.
*Prologue intended for All for Love Reviv'd*, 50, 95.
*Prologue Intended for the Players at Hampton Court*, xviii, 49, 94, 101.

*Prologue Spoken at the Sensorium on His Majesty's Birth-day*, 69, 108.
*Prologue to The Conscious Lovers*, 121 (Welsted), 122.
*Prologue to The Distrest Mother*, 46-47, 93, 99, 108.
*Prologue to The Funeral*, 39, 91.
*Prologue to The Lying Lover*, 41, 91, 102.
*Prologue to The Mistake*, 43, 92.
*Prologue to The Tender Husband*, 92.
*Prologue to the Town* (Steele), 116.
*Prologue to the Town* (Welsted), 96.
*Prologue to the University of Oxford*, xx, 45, 92-93, 99, 100, 101.
*Prologues and Epilogues Celebrated for their Poetical Merit*, 91, 92.
Prologues, fragments of, 117-18.
*Publications of the Modern Language Association*, 97.
Pulteney, Daniel, 119.
Purcell, Daniel, 20, 80, 81, 82, 83, 84, 85, 86.
Purcell, Henry, 80.

Racine, J. B., *Andromaque*, 47, 93.
Ralph, James, *Miscellaneous Poems by Several Hands*, 115.
Ramondon, Lewis, 84.
Rauzzini, Venanzio, 86, 88.
Reed, E. B., *Songs from British Drama*, 85.
Revett, Edmund, 99.
Rhymes in Steele's plays, 57-58, 97.
Rich, John, 51, 96, 116.
Richardson, William, 119.
Ritson, Joseph, *A Select Collection of English Songs*, 81, 88, 119.
*Robin, The* (*Orpheus* III), 83, 86.
*Robin's Complaint*, 85.
Rochester, John Wilmot, Earl of, *Allusion to Horace: Satire I. 10*, xvi; *A Letter from Artemisa in the Town to Cloe in the Country*, xv, 111.
Roscommon, Wentworth Dillon, Earl of, 89, 109.
Rowe, Nicholas, xiv, 53; *Tamerlane*, 53, 96, 111.

S, Mr., 98, 100.
*Satyr against Wit* (Blackmore).

Scheffer, John, *History of Lapland*, 119.
*School of Action, The*, see Steele.
Sedley, Sir Charles, xvi, 76, 100.
*Select Collection of English Songs, A* (Ritson).
*Select Collection of Poems, A* (Nichols).
*Select Epigrams*, 90.
*Select Epigrams of Martial* (Hay).
Selwyn, Mrs. (?) Albinia, 31, 88.
Selwyn, Colonel William, 88.
Shakespeare, William, xv, 46, 52, 93, 96, 103.
Sheppard, Sir Fleetwood, 76, 100.
*Short View of the Immorality and Profaneness of the English Stage, A* (Collier).
Simpson, John, 87.
*Sixth Ode of Horace Apply'd to the Duke of Marlborough, The*, xxii, 14, 78, 101.
Smalwood, James, 11, 75.
Smith, Christopher, the younger, 119.
Smith, David Nichol, *The Oxford Book of Eighteenth-Century Verse*, 89.
Smith, John Stafford, *A Chearful Glee*, 81; *A Collection of Songs of Various Kinds and for Different Voices*, 80.
Smith, William, 85.
Solly, Edward, 75.
*Some Account of the Taylor Family*, 97.
Somers, John, Lord, 4, 74.
*Song* (from the *Muses Mercury*), xvi, 33.
*Song* (from *Town-Talk*), 35, 91.
*Song, A* (from the *Lover*), 114.
*Song, A* (from the *Spectator*), 114.
*Song in The Conscious Lovers, A*, xvii, 26, 86-88.
*Song to Celia's Spinett, A*, 82.
*Songs and Lyrics from the English Playbook* (Boas).
*Songs Compleat, Pleasant and Divertive* (D'Urfey).
*Songs. Francis Hopkinson His Book* (Hopkinson).
*Songs from British Drama* (Reed).
*Songs from the Restoration Theatre* (Thorp).

*Songs in the Comedies Called As You Like It and Twelfth Night* (Arne).
Songs in *The Funeral*, 19–22, 80–82, 99.
Songs in *The Lying Lover*, 21–23, 82–83.
Songs in *The Tender Husband*, 23–26, 83, 86.
*Songs of Thomas D'Urfey, The* (Day).
Sotheby, Messrs., of London, 117.
*Spectator, The, see* Steele.
Spenser, Edmund, *The Faerie Queene*, xv.
*Spleen, The* (Winchilsea).
Steele, Elizabeth, 115.
Steele, Eugene, 97.
Steele, Lady, 107, 111, 113.
Steele, Richard, interest in seventeenth-century poets, xv; admiration for Waller, xv, xvi, xvii; encouragement of contemporary poets, xiv; attitude towards his own verse, xiii, xvii, xviii; desire for anonymity, xviii, 101; first appearance of his poems, xx; reprintings, xx, xxi; revisions, xxiii, 74, 77, 92, 94; stylistic peculiarities, 99–100, 101–2, 103, 106–7, 108, 112, 113, 115; slender reputation as a poet, xxii, xxiii; *The Christian Hero*, xv, xix, 78; *The Funeral*, 80, 99; prologue, 39, 91; songs, 19–22, 80–82, 99; rhymes, 57, 97; epilogue, 40–41, 91; *The Lying Lover*, 82, 99; prologue, 41, 91, 102; songs, 21–23, 82–83; rhymes, 57, 97; epilogue, 41–42, 91; 107; *The Tender Husband*, 15, 80, 83, 99; songs, 23–26, 83–86, 100; rhymes, 57, 97; epilogue, 42–43, 91, 103; *The Tatler*, xiv, xv, xvii, 89, 103, 104, 111, 113; *The Spectator*, xiv, xvii, 74, 89, 92, 93, 114, 119; *The Guardian*, xiv, xix, 79, 89, 104, 105, 114, 119; *The Englishman*, xiv, xix; *An Account of the State of the Roman Catholick Religion*, 120; *Poetical Miscellanies*, xvii, xviii, xix, 74, 77, 102, 103, 106, 107, 111; *The Lover*, xv, 102, 105, 114; *Town-Talk*, xiv, xx, 91, 108,

114; *The Theatre*, xx, 86, 87, 88, 94, 95, 98, 103, 105, 117; *The School of Action*, xvi, 58, 118; *The Conscious Lovers*, 86, 101, 115, 122; *Indiana's Song*, xvii, 26, 86–88; *Epistolary Correspondence (see* Nichols); *Correspondence* (1941), 75, 97, 111, 113, 123.
Stepney, George, 76, 100.
Sterling, James, 122.
Stevens, R. J. S., 88.
Suckling, Sir John, *A Soldier*, xv; *Upon Two Sisters*, xv.
Sullivan, Mr., 84, 85.
Sutherland, James, 104.
Swift, Jonathan, xix, 74, 111, 115, 122; *A Description of the Morning*, xiv; *A Description of a City Shower*, xiv; *The First Ode of the Second Book of Horace Paraphras'd: and Addressed to Richard St—le, Esq.*, 74. The Pope–Swift *Miscellanies* (1728–32), 74, 104.
*Syren, The*, 81, 82, 83, 85, 86.

T., S., 101.
Tate, Nahum, 89, 109.
*Tatler, The, see* Steele.
Taylor, William, *Manuscript Verse Book*, 97.
*Tender Husband, The, see* Steele.
*Term Catalogues* (ed. Arber), 73, 113.
*Theatre, The* (farce), 116.
*Theatre, The, see* Steele.
Thomson, James, 115.
Thorp, Willard, *Songs from the Restoration Theatre*, 80.
*Thrush, The* (*Orpheus* II), 81.
Tickell, R. E., *Thomas Tickell and the Eighteenth-Century Poets*, 95.
Tickell, Thomas, xix, xxii, 79, 95, 108, 111, 120; *Oxford. A Poem*, xxii; *A Poem on the Prospect of Peace*, 107; *Works of Addison*, 79, 120.
*To a Lady on her Parrot*, 113.
*To a Painter: How to Paint His Beloved*, 114.
*To a Young Lady Who Had Marry'd an Old Man*, xvi, 31–33, 89, 102.
*To Belinda*, xvii, 65, 102.

*To Benjamin Hoadly, Bishop of Bangor,* 57, 97.
*To Captain S. on His Poetry* (Bishop).
*To Celia's Spinet,* 21.
*To Congreve on the Way of the World,* xvi, xix, xxii, 12 ff., 76, 98.
*To Flavia,* 65, 102.
*To His Various Mistress,* 85.
*To Mrs. Manley,* 57, 97.
*To My Lov'd Tutour Dr. Ellis,* 14, 78.
*To Serena: on Presenting Her the Conscious Lovers,* 115.
*To Sir Richard Steele. On his Comedy, the Conscious Lovers* (Lewis).
*To the Mirrour of British Knighthood,* 11, 75.
*To the Queen; upon the Death of His Royal Highness,* 111–12.
*Toasts for the Kit-Cat Club,* 35, 90.
Tonson, Jacob, the elder, xix, xx, 76, 77, 78, 79, 80, 83, 92, 106, 107, 111, 113.
*Town-Talk, In a Letter to a Lady in the Country, see* Steele.
*Twelve Arietts or Ballads* (Hayes).

*Universal Harmony,* 85.
*Upon Mr. Steele's Incomparable Elegy on the Death of Queen Mary,* 74.

Vanbrugh, Sir John, 44, 92; *The Provok'd Wife,* 92; *The Mistake,* 43, 92.
*Verses on Mrs. Selwyn, Being Valentine,* 31, 88, 99.
*Verses to the Author of the Tragedy of Cato,* 15, 79, 99.
*Verses Written for the Toasting-Glasses of the Kit-Kat Club in the Year 1703,* 110.
Victor, Benjamin, *Epistle to Sir Richard Steele, on His Play Called the Conscious Lovers,* 112; *Epilogue to The Conscious Lovers,* 122.
Villiers, Edward, Viscount, 5, 74.
Virgil, 69, 73, 117.
*Vocal Magazine, or Compleat British Songster, The,* 81, 82, 88.
*Vocal Miscellany, The,* 82, 85.
*Vocal Poetry* (Aikin).

W., W., 109.
Waller, Edmund, xvi, xvii, 98; *Under a Lady's Picture,* xvi; *Of Love,* xvi; *Upon the Death of My Lady Rich,* xvi; *The Battle of the Summer Islands,* xvi; *Of the Marriage of the Dwarfs,* xvi; *For Drinking of Healths,* xvi; *On My Lady Isabella Playing on the Lute,* xvi.
Walsh, John, xx, 80, 82, 83, 84.
Walton, Clifford E., *History of the British Standing Army 1660-1700,* 73.
*Warbling Muses, The,* 81, 83, 84, 85, 86.
Ward, James, xix, 122.
Watts, Isaac, xiv.
Watts, John, 84.
*Weekly Packet, The,* 108, 120.
Welsted, Leonard, xiv, 90, 96; *Ode for the Prince's Birthday,* 115; *Prologue to the Town,* xx, 96; *Prologue and Epilogue for The Conscious Lovers,* 122; *Epistles, Odes, &c.,* 115.
Wharton, Anne, 77, 98.
Wharton, Philip, Duke of, 115.
Whitlock, John, 73.
Wilks, Robert, 39, 46, 68, 82, 91, 92, 93, 94, 95, 106, 120.
William III, King of England, 3, 7, 13, 20, 51, 54, 74, 97.
Will's Coffee House, 75, 113.
Winchilsea, Anne Finch, Countess of, xvi, xix; *The Spleen,* xvii; *A Pastoral Dialogue between Two Shepherdesses,* xvi, 111.
*Wit and Mirth or Pills to Purge Melancholy* (D'Urfey).
Wolley, E., 101.
Wolseley, Robert, 76, 98.
Wood, Anthony à, 93.
Wood, Robert à, 93.
*Works of Horace in English Verse, The* (Duncombe).
*Works of the British Poets, The* (Anderson).
*Works of the Most Celebrated Minor Poets, The,* xxi.

Young, Edward, xiv, xix, 79.
Young, Isabella, 87.
Younger, Elizabeth, 108.

PRINTED IN
GREAT BRITAIN
AT THE
UNIVERSITY PRESS
OXFORD
BY
CHARLES BATEY
PRINTER
TO THE
UNIVERSITY